# DOES MY CHILD HAVE A DEVELOPMENTAL DELAY?

# Other Books by Sarah Taylor Vanover

*Finding Quality Early Childcare: A Step-by-Step Guide for Parents about What Matters Most* (2016)

*Sticky Situations: Case Studies for Early Childhood Program Management* (2016)

*The Beginnings of School Readiness: Foundations of the Infant and Toddler Classroom* (2017)

# DOES MY CHILD HAVE A DEVELOPMENTAL DELAY?

## A Step-by-Step Guide for Parents on Early Intervention

### Sarah Taylor Vanover

ROWMAN & LITTLEFIELD
Lanham • Boulder • New York • London

Published by Rowman & Littlefield
An imprint of The Rowman & Littlefield Publishing Group, Inc.
4501 Forbes Boulevard, Suite 200, Lanham, Maryland 20706
www.rowman.com

Unit A, Whitacre Mews, 26-34 Stannary Street, London SE11 4AB

British Library Cataloguing in Publication Information Available

**Library of Congress Cataloging-in-Publication Data**

Names: Vanover, Sarah Taylor, author.
Title: Does my child have a developmental delay? : a step-by-step guide for parents on early
    intervention / Sarah Vanover.
Description: Lanham, Maryland : Rowman & Littlefield, 2019.
Identifiers: LCCN 2018014481 (print) | LCCN 2018032251 (ebook) | ISBN 9781475842036
    (ebook) | ISBN 9781475842029 (cloth : alk. paper)
Subjects: LCSH: Learning disabled children—Education (Early childhood) | Slow learning chil-
    dren—Education (Early childhood) | Early childhood education—Parent participation.
Classification: LCC LC4704 (ebook) | LCC LC4704 .V38 2019 (print) | DDC 371.9/0472—dc23
LC record available at https://lccn.loc.gov/2018014481

♾ ™ The paper used in this publication meets the minimum requirements of American National Standard for Information Sciences Permanence of Paper for Printed Library Materials, ANSI/NISO Z39.48-1992.

Printed in the United States of America

To my good friend, Jenna, who is an amazing mother!

# CONTENTS

# FOREWORD

As I share my thoughts, you will see that my perspective is from multiple lenses. As an administrator of a high-quality, inclusive, early care and education center, I spent most of the 1990s working with families as they sought care for their young children, with and without disabilities. The following decade, I was a developmental interventionist, providing support to families with young children with special needs, and currently, as an associate professor of interdisciplinary early childhood education, I teach and support the very students that will become developmental interventionists. But most importantly, I am—and will always be—Mason's mom, a parent who *received* support from early intervention services.

Mason, a now twenty-two-year-old young man with multiple disabilities, introduced me to the field of early intervention. As my world became one of doctors, specialists, and lots of worry, I had to learn how to navigate through the early intervention system, the host of medical specialists, and the many emotions that were part of this new world. However, there wasn't a book to guide me through the process, acronyms, or emotions that came with my precious son. So, as most families do, I had to learn on the fly, which, by definition, suggests learning quickly, while in the middle of a process or decision, and without proper planning and consideration.

As a professional in the field of early childhood, I am grounded in the research base that tells us we learn by doing as we strive to make sense of our experiences and that with each experience, we learn more and build on what we have learned until we finally master the task at hand.

When considering the overwhelming amount of information, people, and processes that come with early intervention, it can take a great deal of time to accumulate the knowledge necessary for navigation. But as Sophia's mom shares in her story, the very nature of early intervention tells us *not* to waste time! The earlier the intervention, the better the outcomes, and who wants to waste time trying to figure out a system when your child's development is at stake?

As you move through the chapters in this book, you will see they are organized in a manner that resembles the order of the family experience: first noticing the differences in your child when compared to other typically developing children, the assessments and meetings that follow, and then the process of referrals and evaluations that can be so very overwhelming. Next comes understanding your child and all that comes with him or her, and finally shedding light on the feelings and emotions that accompany this experience.

Some of the topics provide information to help navigate the process, giving a sense of confidence and understanding, rather than getting lost in all the professional jargon and a process flow that at times seems too fast, and other times may seem slow. But even more important is understanding that the feelings and emotions experienced—any and all of them—are normal. To further this point, following each topic is a family story in which they openly share their experiences, feelings, and emotions. With each story readers can see they are not alone—there really is someone who understands.

The author of this book has experiences in the early intervention arena that she has translated into a family-friendly set of topics that will support individuals as they begin the journey, providing answers to the basics of early intervention. That is not to say that one book will prepare a family for each unique individual child's early intervention experience, but it can indeed prepare a family for an early intervention system, and allow time to plan and prepare.

What is most exciting about this book is that it not only prepares families for the system and process but also demonstrates the value of informal supports, such as families sharing with families. And most important, it provides a framework for allowing, understanding, and working through the emotions that many experience as they cross the threshold of the early intervention system.

I realize that my story and journey resemble those found in this book, and I am so inspired to see families supporting one another by sharing their very personal experiences. It is my hope that you find empowerment and guidance within each chapter. Thank you to the author, Sarah Taylor Vanover, and all the families that shared their stories.

From one parent to another,

Julie Harp Rutland, PhD
Assistant Professor, Early Childhood,
Elementary, and Special Education
Morehead State University

# PREFACE

I have worked in the field of early childhood education for over nineteen years now, and during that time period, I have watched so many families struggle with how to help their children overcome a developmental delay. There are so many emotions attached to this process. Many parents may initially suspect that something is not normal with their child's development, but after that point, they don't know how to help. For years I have been contacted by parents I may have only met one time, but they knew I worked in the field of early childhood special education. They contacted me to ask questions about what to do next because they were so confused.

As a classroom teacher and an administrator, I have sat in hundreds of meetings where I shared evaluation information with a family and then told them I have concerns about the child. I have seen parents experience every emotion from being overwhelmed with the information I have provided to becoming angry when I have offended the family members with the information I shared with the parents. Some families may not have even fully understood the information I shared with them during that time period. It is such a difficult process to explain to the family, especially when they do not suspect any problems themselves.

For many years I have been motivated to help families through the struggle and pain of the early intervention process. I have wanted to be there to help them cope with the emotions of this situation, and I have wanted to help them fight through the tedious steps to secure the special education their children need. I have wanted to help families because I am a special educator, but my story started long before I became a classroom teacher.

## MY STORY

I was an extremely healthy child when I was young. My mother always brags that outside of well-child checkups, she only had to take me to the doctor a handful of times when I was very young. When I hit adolescence, all of that changed.

At first we noticed in middle school that I was having huge fluctuations with my blood sugar that resulted in me passing out. This happened several times at school or in church, and it scared my parents a great deal. Within a few weeks we traveled to a children's hospital in the closest big city, and we spent a week there with the pediatric endocrinologist. He did tests each day to see how low my blood sugar was dropping, and during that week my mother slept on a cot in the hospital room.

Each time the doctor came into my hospital room, my mother pelted him with a long list of questions about what the test showed, what the next steps would be, and if she should be worried yet. The doctor always told her not to worry yet, but that is not what I saw happen. While I was in my hospital bed at night, I heard her crying, and when she spoke to my father each day on the phone, she worried about the possible diagnosis along with the cost of the medical bills. The doctor who sent us home at the end of the week asked that I follow a diabetic diet in order to keep my blood sugar at a normal level.

Then, several years later, more problems arose. At sixteen years old, I had my first grand mal seizure. I was rushed to the emergency room, and the doctors began more testing. The doctors told my mother that many children have one seizure and never have another, so they can't make a diagnosis after just one seizure. When I had my second grand mal seizure four months later, it resulted in a diagnosis of epilepsy.

My mother and father, once again, began doing everything they could to help me. They took me to Washington University Hospital in St. Louis to see a pediatric neurologist and confirm the diagnosis that we received in our small town. They spoke with my teachers and my school about how best to help me as I began taking seizure medication for the first time, and they fought with the health insurance company to get my medical bills and my medication covered by our insurance plan. I watched both of them worry about if I would be able to leave our small town to attend college.

While my parents attempted to take care of me, I was trying to figure out my condition on my own. The doctors were telling me I needed to take my medication every day, get enough sleep each night, limit my caffeine intake, and maintain my blood sugar levels so it would not dip too far below normal. As an adolescent, I truly believed I was invincible and that my doctors and my parents were being overprotective. I rebelled against taking my medication regularly, stayed up late like a typical teenager, and drank Mountain Dew at almost every opportunity.

Sometimes I was fine and had no negative side effects, and sometimes my poor choices resulted in another seizure. The biggest inconveniences of having a seizure were losing my driver's license for ninety days at a time and having others see these embarrassing moments. I was mortified for a few days after the seizure, but I did not remember those emotions long enough to keep healthy habits.

It took me years to learn to take care of myself properly and acknowledge that I had a disability that needed treatment. During that time period, I continued to worry my family, especially since I left our small town to attend college.

As an adult I have finally learned how to take care of myself properly. I have also learned that I have to make certain accommodations to maintain my health. Even when I am busy in day-to-day life, I have to make time to attend doctors' appointments. I also have to make sure I take my medication every day and get regular sleep in order to not place myself at risk of having a seizure. I have had to humble myself and let those around me know about my disability and share information with them about what to do if I were ever to have a seizure around them while I am at work or out with friends.

I was not diagnosed with a disability until I was a teenager, and even though I was old enough to understand the situation and follow the doctor's recommendations, I know my family was terrified about my health and scared about how to take care of me. I wish I could have kept that fear and confusion from my parents. I think it would have been even more terrifying if I was a very small child and my parents watched me suffer from an equally difficult condition. I have so much compassion for families that are going through the evaluation and special education process because I have watched my own family experience a similar situation.

As I began working with students in the early childhood special education classroom, I experienced so much empathy for the families that I interacted with each day because I remember how scary it was to be diagnosed with a disability and to learn to live with that condition. When parents of a preschool-age child asked me questions about what would happen to their child in the future, I often shared my own story of success despite being diagnosed with a disability as a teenager.

## CHANGING MY PERSPECTIVE

After fourteen years of being a teacher and an administrator working with young children, my perspective on early childhood education changed again. When my two-year-old son began to show signs of a developmental delay, I experienced the same confusion and sadness that so many other parents experience when going through the evaluation process. I know exactly how to assess a child for a developmental delay, but even though I knew the steps to help my child, the emotions still seemed extremely powerful at times. I often wondered how parents who had no experience with the early intervention process could deal with both the emotions of being a parent and the confusion of the early intervention process at the same time.

I felt that parents and families needed more information about how to determine if their children had a developmental delay. I found occasional blog posts and online checklists about how to deal with this process, but I could not find one book or resource that walked parents through the entire process.

I also have noticed, with the parents I have helped and in my own personal story, that the path of early intervention can be very lonely. As families process their emotions, they may not be able to share their situation with family members and friends yet. If they do feel comfortable talking to people close to them, they still may not know others who have had similar experiences.

Families need to know that others have been through this process and they are not alone. I wrote this book not only to walk families through the early intervention process but to also bring real-life family stories to others who may feel completely isolated during their introduction to early intervention and special education. This book includes seven different stories of families that went through the evaluation and early intervention process, including my own. I hope these stories will help other families know that it is possible to be successful and supported while helping your child get all the support he or she needs to grow and develop.

# 1

# NOTICING DIFFERENCES

Every child is unique and develops at his or her own pace. That is one of the amazing parts of watching young children grow and learn. Every child is an individual. They each have their own strengths and weaknesses. Even children raised in the same home by the same parents are going to have distinctly different traits. Pediatricians will frequently tell parents not to compare siblings for this very reason. It is essential to acknowledge that each child has a right to be different.

Even though parents expect each child to be unique, there is a point in time when it may be hard to determine if a child is simply showing his individual differences or if that child is struggling with his development. There is a delicate balance between allowing each child the time to develop at her own pace and making sure she does not fall too far behind developmentally before seeking help.

## CHILD DEVELOPMENT PRINCIPLES

Some children are born with a diagnosed disability, and the family already knows that the baby will need extra support. Other children appear to be developing typically, but then a parent or teacher starts to notice small characteristics that make them concerned about the child's development. Although it is always important for parents to follow their instincts about their child's well-being, there are certain rules about child development that are very important to keep in mind.

1. *Each developmental milestone should occur within a flexible window of time, not just a specific date.* For example, it is typical to expect a toddler to begin walking at the age of twelve months, but the normal developmental window for walking is actually nine to sixteen months of age.

2. *Although developmental milestones can occur at different points in time for each child, they typically follow a sequence.* For example, when babies become mobile, first they crawl, then they pull up to a standing position, then they take steps while holding onto the furniture, and finally they take their first steps independently. When developmental milestones occur out of order, for example, if a child walks before crawling, then it may be time to take a closer look at the child's overall development.

3. *Typical development also occurs from head to foot (cephalocaudal) and from the middle to the outer parts of the body (proximodistal).* This means babies will develop control of their head and upper body before they learn to walk. Likewise, young children gain muscle control of their core muscles first, so they learn to roll and sit up before they develop refined hand control.

4. *Development always moves from simple to the complex.* Early social skills may start with an infant making eye contact and smiling, but this will progress toward strong and secure attachments with loving caregivers. In order for a child to achieve complex developmental skills like problem-solving and advance language development, they must achieve simple skills first.

5. *There are sensitive periods of time when children best learn certain skills.* For example, the sensitive period for learning-language skills is approximately eighteen months to three years of age. During this time period, the child's brain is wired to learn language at a much quicker rate than at any other point in development. If a child does not have the opportunity to learn language skills during this time period, it does not mean he will never learn language skills, but it may be more difficult to learn those skills at a later time period.

6. *There are multiple areas, or domains, of development: cognitive development, motor development, social and emotional development, language development, and self-help/independence skills.* These areas of development all overlap with one another, so it is

very difficult to look at each area individually without looking at the whole child.

7. *Children learn through play and exploring their environment.* Young children learn through their senses, so they must have the opportunity to touch, taste, smell, hear, see, and experience their environment in order to learn.

8. *Children develop best when their basic needs are met.* Basic needs include food, water, sleep, medical care, and a safe place to live. It is also a basic need for a child to feel safe and loved. When a child has all of these foundational needs met, then she is ready to move on to higher levels of learning and development.

9. *Child development is affected by a child's genetic composition and by the environment in which the child is growing and learning each day.* Both genetics and environment play an important role in a child's success. A child can be perfectly healthy, but he may not excel if he is not able to explore his environment. At the same time, a child with a disability can advance a great deal if she is in a stimulating learning environment with caretakers that constantly interact with her.

10. *Adverse experiences during early childhood (e.g., poverty, abuse, or living in a home with primary caregiver with a mental illness) can have a profound effect on a child's development.* Early life experiences are a foundation for learning and development, so stressful experiences at a young age can definitely make an impact.

## DEVELOPMENTAL MILESTONES

Along with understanding the general concepts of child development, it can be very helpful for parents to know basic developmental milestones for young children so parents can see if their children have typical skills for their age. Again, these milestones are *estimates* because every skill has a window of time during which a child should have mastered the skill.

## A two-month-old child can

- Smile at people
- Self-soothe for short amounts of time by sucking on his fist or with a pacifier
- Make cooing sounds
- Turn head toward sounds, particularly a parent's voice
- Pay attention to faces
- Begin to follow objects with her eyes
- Recognize familiar people from a distance
- Begin showing disinterest by fussing or crying
- Hold head up and start to push up when lying on tummy

## A four-month-old child should

- Sit up straight if propped up
- Play when lying on her stomach
- Raise his head at a ninety-degree angle when placed on his stomach
- Be able to roll from front to back
- Hold and let go of an object
- Play with a rattle when an adult places it in his hands
- Be able to grasp a rattle with both hands
- Be able to place objects in his mouth
- Make cooing sounds
- Laugh out loud
- Anticipate feeding when he sees a bottle
- Demand attention by fussing
- Recognize parent's voice or touch
- Increase eye contact with familiar adults

## A six-month-old child

- Rolls over in both directions (front to back, back to front)
- Begins to sit without support
- Supports weight on legs and bounces when standing (with support)
- Rocks back and forth on hands and knees
- Crawls backward before moving forward

- Knows familiar faces and begins to identify strangers
- Likes to play with familiar adults
- Responds to other people's emotions
- Imitates sounds
- Strings vowels together when babbling
- Responds when he hears his own name
- Makes sounds to show when she is happy and when she is upset
- Begins to say simple consonant sounds ("m," "b")
- Looks at objects that are close by
- Brings items to her mouth to explore
- Shows curiosity about things
- Tries to grasp objects that are out of reach
- Begins to pass things from one hand to the other

## A nine-month-old child

- Places her hands in front to protect herself from falling
- Crawls
- Sits for extended periods of time
- Pulls himself up to a standing position
- Reaches out for objects while she is still sitting
- Bangs toys together
- Grasps objects between the tip of his thumb and his index finger
- Feeds herself using her fingers
- Responds to simple commands
- Responds to his name
- Understands the meaning of "no"
- Imitates speech sounds
- Plays interactive games such as peek-a-boo and pat-a-cake
- Waves goodbye
- Throws and shakes toys to explore how they work
- Has separation anxiety and may be clingy with parents
- Understands that objects still exist, even when he can't see them (object permanence)

## A twelve-month-old child is expected to

- Stand independently
- Walk alone or walk when holding someone's hand
- Sit down without help
- Bang two blocks together
- Understand how a book works and flip several pages of the book at a time
- Begin pretend play (such as pretending to drink from a cup)
- Follow a fast-moving object
- Help the adult when getting dressed (raises arms)
- Play simple back-and-forth ball games
- Point to objects with her index finger
- Develop an attachment to a stuffed animal or toy
- Make brief trips away from parents to explore familiar environments
- Respond to his name
- Say mama, papa, and at least one or two other words
- Understand simple commands
- Try to imitate animal sounds
- Connect objects with labels

## An eighteen-month-old child

- Runs awkwardly and falls frequently
- Can climb onto small chairs without help
- Walks up stairs while holding on with one hand
- Can build a tower with two to four blocks
- Can use a spoon and cup with assistance
- Can scribble with a crayon
- Listens to a short story and looks at pictures in a book
- Can say ten or more words
- Identifies one or more body parts
- Understands and is able to point to common objects
- Often imitates others
- Is able to undress (e.g., socks, shirt, etc.)
- Frequently uses the word "my" and feels possessive of items around him
- Shows affection frequently

- Has separation anxiety

## A two-year-old child

- Can turn one page at a time when looking at a book
- Can build a tower with six or seven blocks
- Can kick a ball without falling over
- Can pick up objects while standing, without falling over
- Can run more smoothly, with a slightly wider gate than older children
- May begin toilet training
- May be able to put on simple clothes without help
- Is able to communicate basic needs like being thirsty or hungry
- Can use two- to three-word sentences
- Can understand two-step command such as, "Pick up your doll and bring it to me"
- Has a vocabulary of about fifty to three hundred words

## A three-year-old child may

- Be toilet trained during the daytime hours
- Briefly balance or hop on one foot
- Walk up stairs independently with alternating feet
- Be able to build a block tower with more than nine blocks
- Be able to copy a circle
- Be able to pedal a tricycle
- Have a vocabulary of several hundred words
- Use three-word sentences
- Count three objects
- Use plurals and pronouns (he/she)
- Ask frequent questions
- Get dressed independently, except for buttons and tying shoelaces
- Have a longer attention span
- Act out elaborate pretend play stories
- Be afraid of monsters or other imaginary characters
- Know his own name and age
- Begin to share toys with friends

- Participate in group play such as building a Lego tower with a friend

## A four-year-old child can

- Hop on one foot without losing balance
- Throw a ball overhand
- Cut out a simple picture using scissors
- Have a vocabulary of more than a thousand words
- Use four- and five-word sentences
- Use the past tense
- Count to four
- Ask lots of questions and be extremely curious
- Sing simple songs and repeat rhymes
- Have a pretend friend
- Begin to have some understanding of time
- Compare and contrast two objects
- Be defiant when overwhelmed by rules or expectations

## A five-year-old child

- Skips, jumps, and hops with good balance
- Can walk heel-to-toe
- Stays balanced while standing on one foot, even with her eyes closed
- Can use simple tools and writing utensils
- Can copy a triangle
- Can use a knife to spread soft foods
- Has a vocabulary of more than two thousand words
- Uses five or more words in a sentence
- Can count to ten
- Knows telephone number and home address
- Can ask and answer open-ended questions (e.g., how and why)
- Will say "I'm sorry" when he makes a mistake
- Has a group of friends
- Likes to imagine and use pretend play
- May tell elaborate pretend stories and try to convince others they are true

Learning the developmental milestones can help parents understand what their children are attempting to learn next. It is also a way for parents to compare the individual child's development to the developmental norm. Again, every child has strengths and weaknesses, so a typically developing child may not achieve every milestone for the current age. When a parent notices that a child is missing many of the age-appropriate milestones, then there may be a reason to pause and examine the situation more closely.

# STORY 1: JACK

Jack was my first child. I had wanted to be a mother since I was five years old, so I was extremely excited when I found out my husband and I were pregnant. I was a high-risk pregnancy due to a diagnosed chronic illness.

Despite my risk factors, my pregnancy was perfect. I was nauseated and tired like most pregnant mothers, but my own health seemed to have no negative effects on my son. He was born at thirty-nine weeks during a scheduled cesarean section delivery, and we left the hospital five days later with a healthy baby boy.

Jack started attending childcare when he was eight weeks old, and even though I was very emotional to go back to work and leave him, he did well in a small classroom with other babies. During most of his first doctor's checkups, I had no concerns, and the doctor gave him a clean bill of health.

As an early childhood education specialist, I frequently give other families advice about raising their children. As an outside observer, I can observe a child's development and assess whether or not the child is typically developing. As a parent, I have never been able to separate the knowledge I have learned in my field from the emotion of looking at my child with a biased mother's perspective.

Once Jack could crawl, and eventually walk, he was always on the move. He would crawl up on the couch and jump off the top of the cushions. If I left the room to get a load of laundry or use the restroom,

I would come back to find him standing on top of the kitchen table getting ready to jump as far off the table as he could fling his body.

When he was eighteen months old, one of his favorite games was to run straight down the hallway and smack his body into his closed bedroom door. He would fly backward onto the carpet and pop back up off the floor to say "I crashed!" Despite the obvious momentum that knocked him down to the floor, he would sit up with the biggest smile on his face. I did not have a brother growing up, but I frequently heard parents use the phrase "he is all boy." Initially, I just thought that Jack was a typical boy with some daredevil tendencies.

As Jack continued to be more and more active, more and more injuries followed. At the beginning, it was just lots of bruises. When I took him in to see the doctor for his two-year-old checkup, I was worried about what the doctor would say about the bruises that covered my son from head to toe. Working in the field of education, I knew that teachers had made social services reports for children that had fewer bruises than my son.

As soon as the doctor came into the exam room, I began explaining why he was covered in bruises. The pediatrician suggested that we count all the bruises that we could see. He stopped when he got to thirty-eight bruises. Then he looked at me and explained that the location of all the bruises showed an active toddler that was jumping or falling forward as he explored the world. He did encourage me to keep an eye on him whenever possible.

Less than a month after Jack turned two years old, he had his first ER visit due to an injury. I was at the hospital myself that day having tests done due to my second pregnancy, and a teacher from Jack's school called to explain that his arm had gone limp and he seemed unable to move it. My husband picked him up from school, and the doctor sent him to the hospital for an X-ray. The X-ray showed that no bones were broken, but Jack had dislocated his elbow. Luckily, this was an injury that required very little treatment. Some of the injuries that he received later required more medical treatments and follow-up care.

After Jack's dislocated elbow, I began to notice some other concerns. In his classroom at school, many of the other two-year-old children had begun participating in table activities such as puzzles, coloring with crayons, and stacking rings. I never saw Jack play with these types of toys. I asked the teachers if he used these types of toys during the day, but they said he only played in the dress-up area or with the large blocks on the floor.

I had never seen him bring home any type of artwork in the two and a half years of being in a childcare program. When I asked the teacher if he ever did any artwork, the teacher told me that they invited him every day to do the classroom artwork, but Jack always refused to participate. The teacher even mentioned that he would get very upset, to the point of tears, if the teacher strongly encouraged him to sit at the table to do a work of art.

By this point, I had a gut feeling that Jack's hand muscles (or his fine motor skills) did not seem to be strong enough to do the same activities as the other children in his classroom. It also seemed that he had a small amount of anxiety when the teachers asked him to complete activities that require more hand strength. There were other activities, such as Play-Doh and finger paint, that Jack would not even touch. All of this made me think Jack had some type of fine motor delay. At the same time, Jack was so active and energetic, it did not seem as if he had the same delays with his large motor movements.

The state of Kentucky has an early intervention system called First Steps that specializes in providing early intervention and support therapies for children under the age of three. The First Steps program is set up so that doctors, specialists, or parents can place a referral and ask for a child to be evaluated for a developmental delay. I contacted First Steps and completed the referral process myself. Within a couple of weeks the evaluation specialist set up a time to come and evaluate Jack, and she also asked me to complete a parent questionnaire about Jack's development. I stressed to the evaluator that I was not worried about his gross motor skills. I was only worried about his ability to use his fingers to do tasks like puzzles.

About two weeks after Jack's evaluation, First Steps contacted me to let me know that Jack's evaluation showed that his fine motor skills were low; however, the developmental assessment that First Steps used had the evaluator average the fine motor skills together with the gross motor skills. That meant the information I was the most worried about did not come across effectively in the evaluation.

At that point, I called First Steps and began to advocate for why they needed to do a separate evaluation for my child's fine motor skills. This involved giving their office a great deal of documentation about my concerns. After reviewing all the information that I provided, First Steps decided to have an occupational therapist use a specialized assessment tool that specifically looked at fine motor skills. When the results of that assessment came back, it showed that my thirty-month-old son was only able to do the fine motor skills of a sixteen-month-old toddler.

When the occupational therapist did her evaluation, she saw several things from her evaluation that I had missed. I had been so sure that Jack's big motor skills were well developed because he was such an active child. The occupational therapist had concerns about Jack's sensory processing system. She felt that many of his energetic and risky behaviors could be because he was seeking sensory input. She was also concerned about his aversion to activities like finger painting and Play-Doh. He was very defensive to some textures, sounds, and other sensory stimuli. Finally, she felt that Jack was showing unnecessary anxiety about completing activities that required fine motor skills. She told me that when she watched him in the classroom it seemed he was anxious to try an activity that he did not think he could do perfectly on his first attempt.

After the therapist did her full evaluation, Jack qualified for weekly occupational therapy through the state's early intervention program. I was ready for Jack to begin therapy, but I also had to sit down with my husband and discuss how we would begin this process. My education background is early childhood special education, so I am very familiar with the early intervention process. My husband has always heard me discuss my profession, but he isn't as familiar with this process as I am. He had noticed Jack struggling with the same issues that I had noticed; however, since Jack was so young, he still believed he would grow out of these behaviors without any additional assistance.

My husband also had a different perspective on special education than I. He was worried that agreeing to occupational therapy would place a label on our child for most of his educational career. As I continued to explain that special education services during preschool could eliminate Jack needing those services later in his school career, my husband eventually agreed to proceed. He trusted me a great deal, and even if he didn't completely see the need for occupational therapy, he knew I was making my decision in Jack's best interest.

Initially I felt a great deal of relief when Jack finally qualified for occupational therapy, but that was just the beginning of the fight. My two-and-a-half-year-old son was struggling to control his emotions and seemed to have uncontrollable energy. His attempts to be a daredevil were not decreasing.

One evening after school, our family went out to dinner with close friends. Their family had a son the same age as Jack, and our boys often played together. When we went to dinner that evening, one of my friends also invited his parents. At dinner that night, not only was I in a restaurant with a two-and-a-half-year-old, but also I was at dinner with a two-and-a-half-year-old that was extremely active, afraid of loud noises, and overly emotional from a long day at school.

If I sat at the table for a total of five minutes the entire evening, I would be stunned. Jack was crawling under the table, screaming when a noise startled him, and crying as soon as he slowed down for a moment to realize how tired he was. I was physically exhausted after an hour-and-fifteen-minute dinner. Jack's playmate sat at the table the entire evening, colored his children's menu, and ate his meal.

As we all got up from the table to leave the restaurant, my friend's mother looked at me and said, "I could never be his grandmother." I was heartbroken that someone would insult my child to my face. I wanted her to know that my child was spirited. I wanted her to understand that my two-and-a-half-year-old had a huge imagination and a large vocabulary. Instead, she saw my out-of-control little boy, and she did not look any further.

Jack's injuries did not stop immediately either. After about eight months of occupational therapy, Jack fractured the growth plate in his shoulder. Again, this injury occurred while he was at school. During nap time, Jack was lying on the floor of his classroom and became bored. He began violently rocking back and forth while lying on his nap mat. While he was rocking himself on the floor, he smacked his shoulder against the bottom of a shelf next to him. Again, I was notified that Jack was hurt and he could not use his arm.

That evening we took Jack to the ER. He was hysterical during X-rays, and the prolonged wait did not calm him down. Once the doctor told us Jack's shoulder was fractured, he gave us a splint and told me to limit his activity. I looked at my very active three-year-old son and thought, *How am I supposed to limit his activity?*

The occupational therapist (OT) continued to work with Jack as he recovered from his shoulder injury, but during that time period, she also began to address his anxiety. Jack was sincerely worried about attempting an activity that he could not do correctly. When he tried to complete a puzzle or hold a crayon, he was instantly emotional because he knew he couldn't do it correctly. Jack struggled with regulating his emotions, another area in which the OT was supporting him.

When he became emotional because he could not make puzzle pieces match up, his reaction did not match the struggle. Jack was never aggressive, but once he became emotional, he was emotional the entire day. For example, if Jack started to cry over something at 9:30 in the morning, then he was highly emotional the rest of the day. When he continued to get emotional, the teacher would ask him why he was so upset. While standing in a puddle of tears, Jack would respond, "I can't stop crying, and I don't know why!"

The therapist's goal was to help Jack slow down his reaction and think through what he was feeling. She was also using social stories to help him with impulse control. To help his physical development, the OT was working on several large motor skills including balance, coordination, stamina, and planning his movements in advance. Although I had thought Jack's large muscle skills were well developed, I just saw him jumping off furniture and playground equipment. I didn't realize he wasn't strong enough to control his motor skills and that he had minimal stamina to continue his bursts of energy.

Our family dedicated a large amount of time to Jack's therapy. When he was under the age of three, the state's early intervention program sent the occupational therapist to Jack's school for his therapy because, due to the amount of time he spent there, it was the natural environment for Jack to receive support services. Once Jack turned three, we began using a private practice occupational therapist and had to use our health insurance to assist with the cost. I was leaving work early at least once a week to take Jack to see his OT.

When the occupational therapist made suggestions of activities that would help Jack increase his motor skills or control his emotions, we had to duplicate those activities at home. This usually involved purchasing certain materials or doing lots of different motor activities with him. I had to plan these therapy activities into our day or they would be forgotten. Since the occupational therapist no longer visited Jack in his classroom, I had to be extremely vigilant about communicating to his teacher what Jack was working on each week with his OT.

As I spent more time working with Jack on some of these motor skill activities, I began noticing that his pre-academic skills were starting to fall behind. Since Jack would not hold a crayon, participate in table activities with letter matching, or practice writing his name, he was not learning his numbers and letters at the same rate as the other children in his classroom. His vocabulary was huge, and he was great at creative problem-solving. He had the ability to be an academic learner, but his anxiety and his fine motor deficit were starting to affect other areas of his development.

When I thought that he only had a fine motor delay, I could compartmentalize those emotions by telling myself that he just had weak muscles in his hands and that would improve. Once academic skills were involved, it became much harder to keep a positive attitude.

I think any parent that goes through these experiences with a child feels a certain amount of guilt. At this point in my journey, my "mom guilt" was reaching its peak. There were so many questions that continuously plagued me. Did I do this to my child? Was it something I did during my pregnancy? Did my health affect Jack's development?

As a working mother, I found even more questions swirling through my head. Should I have stayed at home with him instead of working and placing him in childcare? Did I put him in a poor-quality childcare program? Am I spending enough time with him outside of work? At the end of a long work day, I often come home exhausted, and I desperately need some rest. Have I ignored my child in my off time?

I also worried about how I was handling the situation now that we knew Jack had a delay. Did I get the best therapist for him? Did I start his therapy soon enough? Was I too busy with my own life to realize my child had these challenges? No matter what questions I asked and obsessed over, there was never a good answer. Every question and every answer led me falling farther down the rabbit hole. I eventually had to decide that I did the best I could by getting Jack the best help I could find as soon as I realized he needed it.

While I struggled internally with my own emotions, I began other battles as well. Once we started to use our health insurance to pay for weekly therapy, I found I had to be a constant advocate for my child. We started the process of using our health insurance with getting a pediatrician referral for Jack needing occupational therapy and by submitting his most recent evaluations to show the areas of his deficits. For a few weeks, this seemed as if it would be enough.

Then I began receiving explanation of benefit (EOB) summaries from our health insurance company that they were declining payment. When I called the insurance company, they initially told me that only children born with a chronic condition (e.g., Down syndrome, cerebral palsy, etc.) needed to receive occupational therapy. With my background in special education, I knew I needed to begin collecting documentation on the benefits of occupational therapy for conditions like sensory processing disorders, fine motor delays, and anxiety. I also collected written statements from teachers and therapists on why Jack needed these services.

I would get to a place with the insurance company that made me think everything was resolved, and then I would receive another EOB denying services. This frustration continued for over six months, and eventually my husband and I made the decision to switch to an occupational therapist that did not bill with insurance and charged a slightly lower hourly rate. The financial sacrifice weighed on us since we had two sons in full-time childcare, but during this transition we found the therapist that helped Jack achieve more goals than anyone else he had worked with up to that point.

Jack's early intervention journey did not only include occupational therapy. We have used multiple resources to help him overcome his obstacles. At two different points Jack has had to see a speech pathologist. The first time he needed speech therapy was around the age of three. At that point Jack was moving so fast all the time that his words often got stuck when he was trying to speak. Speech pathologists often diagnose this problem with fluency.

Jack would be in a huge hurry to tell a story, and he would get stuck on one word, repeating it over and over again. This was different from stuttering. When a child stutters, he will say the same sound over and over and not complete the full word. Jack was completing the full word (and pronouncing it correctly); however, he seemed like a record that would skip and repeat the same part of the song again and again. The speech pathologist told us Jack was moving and thinking so fast that he could not complete his thoughts. She spent about three months working with him on how to slow down when he speaks. After that, he was temporarily discharged from speech therapy.

Several years later Jack would need speech therapy again, but this time it was for a more academic reason. Since Jack had avoided learning his letters and numbers during preschool, he started kindergarten slightly behind the rest of the class. Another talented speech and language pathologist (SLP) began working with him on identifying letter sounds and blended sounds with his beginning reading work at school. Once a week Jack received coaching from the SLP, and then we would work on those same skills during the week.

We also tried some alternative therapies. When Jack was five, we began working with a music therapist that started adapted piano lessons with Jack. The object of the lessons was primarily to develop finger strength and coordination, but the musical skill development was a bonus. The OT also suggested that we get Jack to participate in athletic activities that work on upper body strength, coordination, balance, and stamina. Her first two suggestions were swimming and martial arts. We tried both of these options. We found a martial arts program that did wonders for Jack's strength, focus, and motor planning. It also taught him to be less impulsive and consider the consequences of his actions. He began swim team in the summer, and swimming greatly improved his stamina and upper body strength.

As an educator, I was determined that Jack needed to have the best teachers to support him through this therapy process, but honestly, I feel that many of Jack's teachers never understood him. As early as when Jack was two years old, I would go to pick him up from school and be greeted with teachers that told me stories about how disappointed they were in Jack's overly exuberant behavior.

When Jack was two years old, he was a biter. As soon as I picked him up from school, the teacher was waiting to tell me how many children he'd bitten that day. I was terrified to come and pick him up because I knew I would be scolded. Once he was older, I felt the teachers just didn't understand how special he was. I also realized that they didn't know how to calm him down when he got upset. Some teachers tried to force him to participate in table activities, and that never ended well.

The first teacher that seemed to understand Jack was Ms. Jillian, his pre-kindergarten teacher. She had been told in advance that Jack didn't sleep and was wild at nap time. On her third day in the classroom she told me she realized Jack was a great sleeper if you could just get him to slow down and relax. I heard this voice in my head say, *That's what I have been telling everyone!* She also figured out very quickly that it did not help to force him to sit down and do pre-academic work. Once Jack began elementary school, he has had fantastic teachers. I know we will not be lucky enough to agree with the teaching style of every teacher he has in his academic career, but I still pray each year that his new teacher will understand how he works and appreciate his strengths and talents.

When my husband and I talk about the people who have made the biggest impact on Jack's development over the past several years, his teachers have only been one part of the puzzle. Of course, my husband and I have been an important piece of this growth process, but there are others we desperately needed in order for Jack to be successful.

Amanda, Jack's occupational therapist, was tough on him, but she celebrated every victory with Jack. She helped him overcome many of his fears. I feel she was the person who really helped him build up his confidence. Once he started to become more confident, it was like a boulder rolling down a hill. The momentum was fantastic!

Another person I feel had a huge role in Jack's development is Master Matson, Jack's martial arts instructor. He treated Jack like any other child in the studio by setting high expectations, but he is a teacher who learns individual traits about the children in order to motivate his students. Jack needs someone to be firm and give him consequences when he does not follow those expectations. He also needs a great cheerleading section, and Master Matson celebrated accomplishments with Jack. He acknowledges Jack's sense of humor and creativity.

When I see teachers and therapists individualize their methods to work with each student, it makes my heart feel full. It makes me feel they understand that my child is just as important as any other child they work with each day. Those are the people I want to work with my children.

I have earnestly worked as hard as I can to help my son learn to grow and develop, but at times it is completely exhausting. Jack needs to move and explore, but there are times when I am just too tired to keep moving at his pace. Those are the days that he ends up getting in trouble a lot. I don't mean to get upset with him, but he is the kind of child that finds unique ways to entertain himself when he gets bored. Sometimes it is normal little boy stuff like playing basketball in the

house even if he knows it is not allowed. Other times it is more complicated.

A few years ago, my family traveled to my hometown for my little
sister's wedding. The adults were getting ready to go to the church, and
Jack was getting bored. He began chasing his little brother around the
living room, and then he accidently threw James onto the couch when
he tagged him. Jack did not have any malicious intent, but his little
brother ended up with a broken collarbone. As Jack has gotten older
and learned to control himself more, these accidents are fewer and
farther between. I can also see that he has sincere remorse when something like this happens, but there are times when he has great difficulty
with impulse control.

Jack turned seven this year, and he was discharged from occupational therapy and speech pathology. He still goes to karate several times a
week, and he is involved in several other sports to keep him active and
strong. At seven years old, he is testing on grade level in math and
reading. Recently, he went to see Santa Claus at the local mall, and
when Santa read Jack's letter, Santa said that Jack had excellent pen-
manship. That one comment felt like a huge success to me.

Even though we have been discharged from therapy, the therapist
called it a "break." These types of sensory disorders and delays don't
typically go away completely. They receive treatment and become con-
trollable, but different life experiences can cause them to need additional therapy at different points in a child's life.

As a mom, I know I have an amazing child. I wish I could show that
to everyone. Jack is so creative. He creates elaborate stories with his
pretend play figures and makes beautiful songs. Ever since he was little,
he has had a huge vocabulary, and he uses all of those words to have
dynamic conversations with children and adults.

Jack is extremely friendly. We can be at the public pool for just
fifteen minutes, and he will introduce me to a new friend he just met
that day. I love how empathetic he can be. One of Jack's greatest traits
is his sense of humor. Our children's pastor at church often tells me that
Jack is a constant entertainer, and you never know what will come out
of his mouth next. I think she enjoys listening to those off-the-wall
comments.

Of course, I know Jack has his faults. We all do. But I see an amazing
young man each time I look at him, and I have complete faith that he

will continue to win people over with his charm, comedy, and compassion. As a mom, I pray those are the characteristics that all people will see when they meet my child.

If I could give advice to other families that are entering the early intervention process, I want to tell them to follow their gut instinct. If you feel your child needs help, then don't stop pushing until someone will listen. Parents also need to know that early intervention can mean the entire family must do a lot of work and make sacrifices such as giving time and energy. It is a commitment to help your child through the early intervention process, but it is so worth it in the end.

# 2

# WHAT IS A DEVELOPMENTAL DELAY?

**W**hen a child under the age of eight years old qualifies for special education, the evaluation summary will typically show that the child has a developmental delay. The child's IEP (Individualized Education Program) does not require the diagnosis to be more specific. The team only needs to identify the reason for special education as a development delay, with no further articulation.

## WHAT IS A DEVELOPMENTAL DELAY?

A developmental delay means that the child is not meeting the developmental milestones (in one or more areas of development) within the expected time period. The developmental delay can be a significant delay or it may be a minor condition that resolves after a short amount of additional therapy and intervention. The delay can be limited to an individual area: cognition, motor skills, language skills, social and emotional skills, or self-help/independence skills. Some children will have delays in a combination of these areas. The Individuals with Disabilities Education Act establishes that a developmental delay means a delay in one or more of the following areas: physical, cognitive, communication, social or emotional, or adaptive development.

It is important to remember that developmental skills typically occur in a predictable sequence; however, each child develops skills on an individual timetable. Developmental milestones usually have a window of time that is considered "on target." One of the most common examples is when a child learns to walk. The average developmental milestone for walking is twelve months, but it is still considered typical for a child to learn to walk between nine and fifteen months of age. If a child is not walking by fifteen months, this may be a red flag that the child needs further evaluation.

When a child is evaluated and classified as having a developmental delay, it does not mean the child is just a little bit slower than his peers at learning new skills. This classification means there is a consistent pattern showing that the child is struggling to meet the developmental milestones for multiple skills. The classification also indicates that the IEP team attempted to make several accommodations for the child, but the child continued to struggle with meeting the developmental milestones. The classification for developmental delay is not issued when a child is only struggling with one specific skill, such as toilet training. The classification is used when there is a specific pattern of delays in the same developmental area.

## WHAT CAUSES A DEVELOPMENTAL DELAY?

There are several different ways a development delay can occur. The predominant reasons include the following:

- *Genetic reasons.* A child is born with a genetic condition like Down syndrome or fragile X syndrome. These genetic conditions place the child at risk for a developmental delay. Even when the child has a genetic illness that causes a predisposition for developmental delays, there is no way to predict the severity of the delay. Some children with genetic conditions may receive special education and early intervention beginning at a very young age, so the condition can be much milder than if the family had waited several years to begin treatment.
- *Complications at birth.* Children who are born with a low birth weight, are deprived of oxygen during the birth process, or are born extremely premature also have a high risk of developmental delays.

- *Environmental factors.* When children are exposed to adverse situations in childhood, it can have a profound effect on their development. Some environmental factors that create high-stress situations for young children include living in poverty, poor nutrition, an unsafe living environment, exposure to harmful agents like lead, and exposure to drugs and alcohol, abuse, and other family trauma. These types of risk factors have a cumulative effect on the child. The more risk factors that the child is exposed to, the more likely it will be for a child to experience some type of delay.

It is easy for a parent to worry that he or she is the cause of a child's developmental delay. That is not typically the case. Even if the child has a genetic condition, it may not be a condition that runs in the family. For example, a child that was born with epilepsy may have no other family members with epilepsy. There are also environmental factors that can be out of the family's control, such as exposure to lead. Regardless of what caused the developmental delay, the most important thing the family can do going forward is to support the child regardless of his or her ability level.

## WHAT IS THE DIFFERENCE BETWEEN A DEVELOPMENTAL DELAY AND A DISABILITY?

Doctors and school systems may occasionally refer to disabilities and developmental delays as similar conditions, but it is important to remember that the two conditions are very different. When a child is diagnosed with a disability like fetal alcohol syndrome, autism, or cerebral palsy, the child will never outgrow that disability. The child can definitely make progress, but a disability is a condition that will stay with the child for life.

Developmental delays can be temporary delays, and with the help of developmental specialists, the child may recover from the delay and begin meeting typical developmental milestones. At the same time, a developmental delay may be the early warning sign that a child has a learning or a behavioral disability that can't be diagnosed in early childhood. Some children still have delays when they are in early elementary school, so at that point, the IEP team may need to do further evaluation to determine if the child has a disability that was not diagnosed at an earlier age.

A delay can be a red flag in early childhood for a larger issue later in life, or it could be a short-term delay that is resolved with early intervention. The term *developmental delay* is still very flexible, and it prevents some children from receiving an inaccurate diagnosis early in their childhood.

Also, a developmental delay typically focuses on one area of development at a time. It is possible for a child to have a developmental delay in multiple areas, but the term itself typically looks at each individual developmental area separately. A disability is a specific condition that may affect multiple domains with one diagnosis. For example, a child with Down syndrome may have developmental delays in cognition, motor skills, language skills, social/emotional skills, and self-help skills. These are all areas typically affected by the one disability. However, a child that has a developmental delay in social and emotional skills may be typically developing in all other developmental areas.

It is important to keep in mind that there are individual developmental areas for every developing child: cognition, language skills, social/emotional skills, motor skills, and self-help skills. Many early education specialists will also include the sensory processing system as a developmental area.

## COGNITIVE DEVELOPMENT

Cognitive delays typically include the function of the brain and intellectual functions. This type of delay can result in the following problems:

- Difficulty communicating with others
- Difficulty understanding and decoding what others say during conversations
- Difficulty learning social rules
- Difficulty with long-term and short-term memory
- Difficulty with making decisions and problem-solving
- Difficulty learning self-help skills that allow the child more independence

The possible causes for this type of developmental delay can include the following:

- Genetic disorders
- Severe medical problems at birth
- Abuse or neglect in early childhood
- Exposure to toxins before or after the child was born
- Different types of learning disabilities
- Unknown causes

Instead of focusing on the cause of the delay, it is essential to begin early intervention as soon as possible. Therapists and early childhood special educators will work with young children to break skills down into one or two simple steps to help them understand the skills and to have small victories. The therapists can also give families specific activities to do at home to help develop a specific set of cognitive skills. It is essential to develop as many cognitive skills as possible at a very early age since cognition overlaps with so many of the other developmental areas.

## LANGUAGE DEVELOPMENT

There are three main types of language skills that every young child is learning and developing: receptive language, expressive language, and pragmatic language. Receptive language is when a child receives language from someone else and processes the information he or she hears. If a child has a receptive language delay, then he is medically able to hear the words that someone is speaking to him, but he does not understand the meaning attached to those words.

Expressive language is how a child uses words to express his or her own thoughts, wants, and needs. When a child has an expressive language delay, it could mean she does not know how to use words to identify her feelings and actions due to a reduced vocabulary or difficulty identifying her own emotions. This type of delay could also mean that the child knows exactly what she wants to say, but the muscles around the mouth, lips, and tongue prohibit the child from articulating the words she wants to use.

An expressive language delay can be very frustrating for a child who knows exactly what she would like to say and becomes agitated when those around her who do not understand her communication. Many children with a language delay may have a combination of receptive and expressive language delays, but it is also common for a child to need assistance only with expressive language articulation.

Pragmatic speech skills are those that help children learn to use communication in the correct social methods. Pragmatics can include the words that a child uses, but it can also include tone of voice, body language, volume of the voice, and whether or not the language is appropriate for the social situation. Many children who struggle with pragmatic skills also have delays in the social/emotional developmental domain.

Speech delays are the most common developmental delay, and it is not uncommon for a child as young as a toddler to be diagnosed with a speech and language developmental delay. The National Institute on Deafness and Other Communication Disorders (2016) states that one in every twelve children between the ages of three and seven has a disorder related to voice, speech, or language. One of the most common causes of a speech delay with very young children is hearing damage caused by frequent ear infections as an infant and toddler. When young children are diagnosed with a series of ear infections, many pediatricians will recommend ear tubes in order to reduce ear infections and prevent any damage to the child's hearing. Other possible causes of speech and language delays include the following:

- Hearing loss due to genetic disorders, medications, or trauma
- Exposure to multiple languages—the child will usually have a delay initially while trying to sort out the two languages, but he or she will typically meet developmental milestones by preschool or kindergarten entry.
- Child abuse or neglect
- A learning disability
- Dysarthria—a problem with the muscles that control speech
- A cognitive delay that makes it difficult for a child to decode speech when he or she hears someone else speaking
- Unknown causes

When a child with a speech and language delay works with a speech and language pathologist (SLP), the SLP can work with the child on language comprehension as well as muscle control for articulation. One key to helping young children improve their speech and language skills is to make sure a parent or older sibling does not speak for the child. When a child is asked a question, it is important for the adult to wait for the child to attempt to respond. If a young child knows that someone else will answer for her, she may have no motivation to speak. Even when adults are in a hurry, they must devote the time to wait for a response and show each child that what he or she wants to say is important.

## SOCIAL AND EMOTIONAL DEVELOPMENT

When a child has a social delay, he or she typically has a difficult time understanding social cues, following social rules, or interacting with other children. Children who have an emotional delay have a difficult time controlling and expressing their own emotions, as well as understanding the emotions of others. Many children with a social/emotional delay have a difficult time with self-regulation, which is the child's ability to control his or her emotions and deal with changes. These delays can affect the child's ability to learn, communicate with others, and interact with both children and adults. When a child has a social/emotional developmental delay, the warning signs typically show up before the child enters formal education; however, it may be harder to identify for children who are never in settings with other children their own age. Possible causes for social/emotional developmental delays can include the following:

- Attachment disorders
- Cognitive delays
- Neglect from a parent or from an early environment such as a foster-care setting
- Ineffective parenting
- Unknown causes

Social and emotional delays are also common for children who have the diagnosis of autism spectrum disorder (ASD). ASD is a pervasive developmental disorder that includes difficulty with communication skills, difficulty with self-regulations, repetitive behaviors, and self-help skills. Most children with autism spectrum disorder will have social and emotional developmental delays, but most children with social and emotional development delays will not necessarily have autism spectrum disorder.

Speech and language pathologists or occupational therapists will typically attempt skill-oriented therapy and utilize tools such as social stories to help children make progress with social and emotional skills. There are some types of social/emotional developmental delays that can be treated with medication, but this would be a decision left up to the family and the child's physician. Just like the other types of developmental delays, it makes a significant impact to begin treatment of social/emotional delays at a young age. Depending on the age of the child and the type of delay, treatment could include play therapy or attachment therapy between the parent and the child.

## MOTOR DEVELOPMENT

When a child has a motor delay it can affect his or her large muscles that move the entire body (gross motor movements) or the small muscles that coordinate hand movements (fine motor movements). Gross motor skills include rolling over, crawling, walking, running, jumping, climbing, and skipping. Fine motor skills include grasping, using a fork and spoon, tying shoes, and using a crayon or pencil to write.

Some motor delays come from diagnosed conditions like cerebral palsy or muscular dystrophy. Large muscle delays can also be attributed to structural problems such as one leg being longer than the other leg. Many fine motor delays occur when the child's gross motor skills are not strongly developed.

One of the basic child development principles states that children develop from the core out to the extremities, so if a child does not have strong core muscles, balance, and coordination, it will be very difficult to develop fine motor skills like coloring with a crayon or placing beads on a string. Possible causes of motor developmental delays include the following:

- Premature birth
- Cognitive developmental delays
- Vision delays
- Ataxia—a condition that impairs muscle coordination
- Cerebral palsy—a condition caused by brain damage before or during birth
- Myopathy—a disease of the muscles
- Spina bifida—a genetic condition that causes partial or complete paralysis of the lower half of the body
- Unknown causes

In most cases, a child with a motor delay will be referred for physical therapy or occupational therapy to help develop strength, balance, and coordination. The doctor may also encourage that the child participate in more physical activity in order to increase strength and stamina. Many physicians and therapists will also encourage parents to stop doing simple activities for their children and encourage them to be more independent. A toddler is less likely to walk if she knows a parent will carry her anywhere she wants to go. It is important the children learn to be independent in their motor skills in order to achieve their goals.

## SELF-HELP SKILLS

Self-help skills are skills that help young children to be independent and take care of their own needs. Self-help skills include feeding, self-soothing, dressing and undressing, toileting, bathing, and grooming skills. Self-help skills begin during infancy when young infants learn to take a bottle or use a pacifier to calm themselves down. When a child is a toddler, families usually focus on undressing, washing hands, and calming down after a tantrum. Preschool students should be able to brush their teeth, go to the restroom independently, dress independently, use a fork at meals, and clean up after themselves.

Children who struggle with self-help skills typically have delays with fine motor skills or social/emotional skills. Self-help skills also require a child to use cognition to make independent choices and learn repetitive patterns. When children are first learning self-help skills, it is important for teachers and family members to help children be successful. For example, when a child first begins to toilet train, it is helpful for the child to wear elastic waistband pants that he or she can get up and down quickly when using the restroom. Once the child is proficient, it will not be as necessary to make this type of accommodation.

Occupational therapists typically have many recommendations for how to help a child be successful at these skills, and they are always willing to share strategies with the family so the child has consistency when she is first learning new and challenging activities. The early childhood years are typically the sensitive time period for children to master these independence skills, so it is critical to work with all children, despite their level of developmental delay, so they can achieve their highest level of mastery.

## SENSORY SYSTEM DEVELOPMENT AND SENSORY PROCESSING DISORDERS

Sensory processing is the way the body takes information in through the senses and then decodes that information in order to decide how to react. In a high-functioning sensory system, the neurological system will take in sensory information, the brain will organize that information so that it makes sense, and then the brain tells the body how to respond. This means information that comes in through the sensory system affects social relationships, motor skills, focus, and problem-solving.

Sensory processing disorder (SPD) exists when the sensory system is not able to accept and decode the information for the body to make a well-informed choice. SPD operates on a continuum, so every case is individualized. Some children only have mild amounts of dysfunction, while other children deal with constant sensory challenges throughout the day that disrupt their normal daily activities.

The body has many different senses that take in information, and they include the following:

- Auditory: the sense of sound. This sense receives information from the ear to recognize, discriminate, process, and respond to sounds.
- Oral: the sense of taste and touch (related to the mouth). This sense receives information from the mouth to recognize, discriminate, process, and respond to all information that enters the mouth.
- Olfactory: the sense of smell. This sense receives information from the nose to recognize, discriminate, process, and respond to odors.
- Visual: the sense of sight. This sense receives information to recognize, discriminate, process, and respond to information collected by the eyes.
- Tactile: the sense of touch. This sense receives information from nerves and receptors all over the skin about temperature, touch, pressure, and pain.
- Vestibular: the sense of movement. This sense receives information from the inner ear about the body moving through space, the body's position in space, gravitational changes, and equilibrium.
- Proprioception: the sense of position. This sense receives information from the muscles and joints about weight, pressure, body position, stretching, and changes in position.

When a child is diagnosed with an SPD it is essential for families to remember that this is a neurological disorder. It is not the behavior of a "bad child" or the result of poor parenting. Because it is a neurological disorder, SPD does require treatment. The child is reacting to very specific sensory input.

During the diagnosis and treatment process, it is essential to determine which sensory systems are affected by the disorder, and it is also important to observe the frequency, the duration, and the intensity of the child's reaction to certain stimuli. All children have a response to sensory information, but it is considered a disorder when the intensity, duration, and frequency of the reaction do not seem to match the stimuli. Just as with other developmental delays, trained specialists like occupational therapists can teach the child and the family strategies to help the child respond to incoming sensory input more typically, but it is also essential that treatment starts at a young age in order to help the child be successful.

## REFERENCE

National Institute on Deafness and Other Communication Disorders. 2016. "Quick Statistics on Voice, Speech, and Language." Last updated May 19, 2016. https://www.nidcd.nih.gov.

# STORY 2: LUKE

## Told by Luke's Father, Winston

Luke's story began long before he joined our family. My wife, Katie, and I had decided several years beforehand that we wanted to adopt. We had a healthy biological daughter, but we saw the need for adoptive parents. We had our minds set on adopting a baby from China. There seemed to be many delays in this process, and after a few years of waiting, we decided that a domestic adoption would be a possibility as well.

We connected with an adoption agency inside our state and initiated the paperwork process. From that point, the adoption went much quicker than we anticipated. After the first time we met with the mother, she selected us, and we only had five weeks to prepare for a new child. That seems like a lot of time initially. A lot can happen in five weeks! But when you realize that the typical biological family has seven to eight months to prepare for a new baby, you then realize that we had very limited time.

Luke's biological parents found out they were pregnant while using birth control, and as soon as they knew they were pregnant, they realized they would not be able to care for him properly. The mother and father already had two children, and the pregnancy seemed to be more than the family could handle. Adoption seemed like the best plan for the baby.

The biological mother was twenty-three years old when Luke was born, and she had grown up in a home with many challenging circumstances. The biological father also had a challenging childhood, and he struggled with depression. During the pregnancy, the father lost his job, and this caused the family to become homeless. Once the family did not have a stable living situation, the two older children were placed in temporary foster care, and the mother began looking for an adoptive family for the child she was expecting.

Despite all the difficulties the family was experiencing, the mother was very resourceful. She selected the adoption agency, and she began the process to find a family for the baby. That is how she connected with Katie and me.

At that point the family was living in poverty, and the mother had limited prenatal care. The adoption agency helped her obtain the right doctor's appointments. Obviously the stress of losing her home and having an unplanned pregnancy had taken a toll on her, but the baby seemed to be completely healthy. The doctor had no prenatal concerns. We did not receive any information about the mother's family medical history, but the doctor assured us that she and the baby were healthy at the time of the examinations.

The day that Luke was born, everything went as smoothly as possible. The mother was able to have a typical birth with no complications and no unplanned C-section. After Luke was born, both the mother and the father wanted to hold him before letting him go to his new adoptive family. This scared us a little. It seemed like it would be impossible to hold the baby in your arms and then pass him over to another family to raise.

His mother stayed in the hospital with him for two days before making the biggest sacrifice that I can imagine. She selflessly said goodbye and gave the baby to the nurse to bring him to us. In retrospect, Katie and I believe it must have taken a great deal of courage to meet him and then say goodbye. We had already agreed to an open adoption at that point, so they would see Luke again; however, the emotions of saying goodbye to him that day must have been overwhelming.

During his infancy, it was very easy to take care of Luke. His older sister had several health complications when she was an infant. Luke was healthy, and he only cried when typical babies cried: when he was tired, when he was hungry, and when we needed to change his diaper.

We had very few doctor visits during his first year. He didn't have any ear infections, and he rarely got sick. We only experienced the typical developmental stages such as when he felt bad due to cutting new teeth. Even that seemed relatively mild.

Once Luke started to crawl and walk, we noticed that he was rough! He just seemed to move through the house like a small bulldozer. Things got knocked down. He ran into things. He got bumps and bruises. People continuously made the comment to us that he was "all boy." Since our first child was a quiet and reserved little girl, we assumed this is what little boys acted like as toddlers. Other people dismissed his accidents and rough movements, so we just started to believe it was "normal."

Somewhere in between a year and a half and two years we realized that something was not normal. Katie is an elementary school teacher, so she started thinking of the possibilities that she had seen in the classroom. She worried about ADHD, oppositional defiancy disorder, or bipolar disorder. I just noticed that he was defiant and that he was having a huge number of temper tantrums. He couldn't sit in a chair more than a moment or two. He didn't like to be anywhere that was loud or that had a lot of commotion.

We couldn't take him to restaurants or out in public, so we started to stay home a lot. We talked to a couple of child psychiatry specialists (that typically worked with elementary students) to ask if we needed to have Luke tested for conditions like ADHD or oppositional defiancy disorder, and all of them told us that you can't do those types of tests on a child as young as Luke. He would have to be older before we considered that type of testing, so we decided to wait and hope that the situation improved.

By the time Luke turned two years old, we were very confused, and our home life was extremely challenging. Luke went to an in-home sitter during the day when Katie and I were at work. She would frequently tell us, "He's so good." We couldn't figure out what was different at her house compared to our house. How was she disciplining him? We weren't able to find a way to discipline his behavior that seemed to make any impact on him. He would just throw another temper tantrum three minutes later.

We often said Luke was born "street smart." He knew how to be cunning from birth. He knew how to work his way around a situation.

My wife and I are definitely not street smart. I am an engineer. I base my learning on facts and data. Luke, on the other hand, has an intuition that allows him to manipulate a situation. Even when we tried to discipline his behavior, he found a way to work around us.

As Luke grew closer to two and a half, we felt he needed more of a challenge than the in-home sitter could give him. We decided to enroll him in the Montessori preschool program that was close to our home. As an educator, my wife has always had a great respect for the Montessori curriculum. Plus, we thought that a hands-on approach to learning would best meet Luke's needs. He could begin the program at two and a half years old, but he had to be toilet trained first.

For several weeks we worked extremely hard to toilet train Luke. As I said, he was extremely smart, but in his particular case, toilet training had more to do with whether or not he wanted to use the toilet than whether or not he was capable. At any rate, he was able to use the toilet by the time he started at the Montessori preschool. We were excited about this new possibility for him.

The Montessori school was not a good experience for Luke. He is a child who needs a great deal of structure, and three hours of daily free choice time was just too much freedom for him. He would purposely decide not to use the restroom at times and have an accident. The teachers tried to eliminate his accidents by requiring him to sit on the toilet throughout the day until he went to the bathroom. With his defiant attitude, this solution did not work. There was one point when he sat on the toilet for forty-five minutes straight and still would not go to the bathroom. We scheduled a conference with the teachers to discuss how he was doing. The conference was painful. The conference was almost an hour-long list of everything that Luke was doing wrong. Nothing she said was positive.

Katie began to dread picking him up from school because she was embarrassed and ashamed of what the teachers would say to us about our son. Then we couldn't figure out what to do with all of that negative information. He was so young that he didn't remember what he had done wrong by the time we got him home from school. Putting him in time-out for something that happened five hours earlier didn't seem as if it would be effective. At the same time, we didn't want this type of behavior to continue, so how were we supposed to punish him?

Eventually we made the decision to take him out of the Montessori preschool program. This was a hard pill to swallow for our family. It brought to light that our son was not flexible enough to be successful in any classroom setting. We had to realize that he did have some specific needs that other children may not have.

There was a childcare program on-site at my work, so we immediately put Luke on the wait list to get a spot there. We had a three- to four-week wait, so we had to put together childcare during that time period. Each set of grandparents offered to come to town and spend a different week with him. We also asked for support from family friends.

Around the same time period, Katie had reconnected with a childhood friend, Heather, on social media, and they had decided to get together for coffee to catch up. During their conversation that day, Katie began to talk about everything that was going on with Luke and how tough it had been on the family. Heather listened very closely.

By trade, Heather is a pediatric occupational therapist. She explained to Katie that although a child does need to be older for a diagnosis like ADHD or ODD, children as young as infants can be evaluated for developmental delays and start receiving therapy to help them overcome the type of challenges that Luke was experiencing. Heather told Katie that she would help us get Luke evaluated and make sure the evaluation was coded correctly so the insurance company would approve occupational therapy for Luke.

Luke began three-year-old preschool at the Bright Horizons childcare program located at my work. Luke slowly began to thrive in his new classroom due to its structure, consistent teachers, positive redirection for discipline (instead of time-out), and the opportunity for him to make his own choices. Once we had been at the preschool for several weeks, we found out that the center partnered with a local pediatric occupational therapy (OT) office. Students that needed OT could be seen in the classroom so that the therapist could see the children in their most natural environment, instead of in a more clinical office setting. Currently, Luke works with the OT that visits his school and an OT that he sees weekly in an office setting that has access to a therapy gym.

The therapists had several initial observations about our son. Luke has a great vocabulary. He has never been a candidate for speech therapy. He is strong and powerful. This can mean he is very forceful at times. Luke is not withdrawn. The OTs really wanted to work on his vestibular system, which means that Luke was having a difficult time understanding where his body is in space and being aware of himself. Many times Luke does not know when he is hurting people. That is frequently when people say that he is "all boy."

Luke thrives on structure. He needs to know what is going to happen next. That is one of the reasons he was excelling so much in his new preschool program. They had a consistent schedule and could tell him the next thing that was going to happen each day.

Along those same lines, Luke struggled during any transition that occurred during the course of the day: cleaning up, getting ready to go outside, getting ready for a nap, and so forth. We have really tried to keep a consistent schedule in our home to help deal with transitions. Unfortunately, my job doesn't always make that possible. I work for a company that is based overseas, and I have to travel out of the country several times a year. I am usually gone for two to three weeks at a time, and then Katie is responsible for keeping our household up and running. During those two- to three-week stretches, the focus of the house shifts from a regular schedule to simple survival. This is when home life can be very challenging for Luke. Luckily, even though our home may have changed its schedule, Luke's preschool is still keeping most of his day consistent.

The occupational therapists never really gave him an official diagnosis. They usually refer to him as an SPD (sensory processing disorder) kid. His body just has a difficult time processing all of the sensory information it is taking in from the environment. I was extremely skeptical about occupational therapy at first. My schedule was more flexible to take him to his weekly OT appointments, so I was the one who got to go and watch him with his therapist each week. It looked as if he was just down on the floor playing. He was swinging on his stomach or riding on a scooter board. These were all toys that we could buy at home. Why were we spending so much money on weekly therapy for normal toys? I was baffled as to why I was paying a professional to play in shaving cream with my son.

Then I began to see the results. Luke's focus began to improve. As he progresses, he is able to do more of the activities that the OT provides for him and he stays engaged longer. He is learning to manage his emotions better. The therapists are helping us pinpoint ways that we can continue to work with Luke at school and at home. Right now we are spending a lot of time telling him to "slow down his engine" because he is always moving faster than he needs to move in his environment.

We have received help from multiple sources throughout this journey. Around the time that Luke was beginning OT, we also went to a pediatrician at our local pediatric practice. We took a stack of notes and documentation that Katie had compiled, and we spent almost forty-five minutes talking to the doctor. He just listened to everything that we had to say and reassured us that we were working toward helping our son.

One of his suggestions was a referral to a behavioral therapist who actually works with parents more than the children. One thing that Katie and I have consistently struggled with during this entire process is how to discipline Luke when he behaves inappropriately. We don't want to punish him too harshly or punish him for something that he doesn't understand. At the same time, it isn't okay for him to misbehave and have no consequences.

This new therapist introduced us to PCIT (parent-child interaction therapy). The purpose was for Katie and me to get on the same page on how to handle some of Luke's more extreme behaviors. The therapist really stressed that if we handle the situations consistently, we will be more apt to reduce the negative behaviors. This is still a learning process for us. We have time periods where we do a great job of being consistent, and then we have other periods of upheaval in our home (such as when I leave the country for three weeks) and consistency is harder to achieve.

Through this whole journey, we have had a lot of support. Our friends have been a huge comfort, but we have been very selective with whom we have shared this information. Katie was very emotional about the situation one day during a church meeting and shared some of what we were dealing with regarding Luke's school situation. Immediately after the meeting, two other mothers, who had been through similar experiences with their own children, began reaching out to her. They told her that this would be tough, but they shared a lot of what they had learned with their children.

My family hasn't asked a lot of questions. They were willing to come and spend a week with Luke after we pulled him from the Montessori preschool program, but due to distance, they aren't involved in everyday life. I think it is hard for them to understand everything that we are dealing with if they aren't here day after day. During the week they were here, they told us each day that Luke was fine as long as he got what he wanted. I think they were trying to reassure us. Being with Luke one-on-one is very different than seeing him in a classroom with lots of other children. I think they just want everything to be okay and not have to acknowledge a problem.

Katie's family lives closer, and they have seen much more of the journey we have been through in the past couple of years. Like myself, they didn't really think he needed occupational therapy originally. Now that they can see the difference in his behavior over the past year, they have become believers in OT. They have even told us that if there was ever a time we couldn't afford it, they would be willing to help. I know they see that it is benefitting him.

In general, I think most people want to be supportive when they see you going through any type of struggle with your child. Being a parent is hard, so most people want to offer solidarity when they see other parents in the trenches. This job is hard! We are still really sensitive to the comments about Luke being "all boy." That is not the problem. There is more going on than the simple truth that he is a boy. I think other parents make that comment because it just allows for excuses instead of focusing on the real issue.

The past couple of years have been very emotional. I am usually the even-tempered parent. I have been the most frustrated when Luke has had tantrums in public places and I am faced with embarrassment. My biggest fear with all of this is that Luke's sensory processing problems will affect his education. To me, education is the foundation for a successful life. Education allows you to master a certain set of skills and be financially stable as an adult.

If Luke is distracted from his education by his sensory processing problems, how will it affect his ability to succeed as an adult? I know he is only four, and he has lots of time to master his delays, but I still think about the possible long-term effects. The public school system has a certain mold that it places each child into in order to learn and be a part of a classroom from kindergarten through high school. I am worried that Luke might not fit into that mold. If he doesn't fit, what will happen? How do we help him learn to be successful, despite that mold?

Katie, on the other hand, has had different worries. She will tell you that her biggest worry has been how to discipline him in a way that he understands and that we can get through to him. I can also see that she is worried about "messing him up." Since she is not Luke's birth mother, she has worried that maybe the birth mother would have instinctually known how to handle Luke better then she does. She has found herself second-guessing her gut instincts frequently during this process.

As a teacher, she knows how to work with all types of students in her classroom. When it comes to her own son, out of a deep love, she wants to handle it perfectly, so she worries about her actions a lot. Inevitably, we are going to make some mistakes. But right now, we both are trying to remind ourselves that we are doing everything we can to help him, and that is what is most important. Sometimes we take two steps forward and one step back, but in the end, we are still moving forward.

When you go through this type of adventure with your child, you naturally focus on so many negatives. The fact is, Luke really has a lot of positives. Luke has a huge vocabulary and he can have complicated conversations. He is extroverted and enjoys being around other people. Although he can be very rough, he has a great deal of compassion for other people, and he adores his big sister, Ava. He is always asking us, "Are you happy? I want you to be happy!" When he is interacting with someone one-on-one, he can be extremely calm and a lot of fun as a playmate.

Luke is extremely intellectual, and he is very mechanically inclined. I love to look at the block structures that he creates and ask about how he decided to build them. Right now one of his favorite toys is Transformers, and he loves the robots with the most complicated pieces. He has the innate ability to move them and create new shapes.

Luke's innocence and awe are two of his most amazing qualities. Recently, Katie took him on a short errand to buy something at Kohl's. As he walked past the area of the store with the toys, he froze in one place and just stared in amazement at all of the items on the shelves. His little jaw fell open, and he was giddy just to see everything in front of him. So many children have lost that sense of wonder, but Luke is always finding small things around him to be amazed by.

Luke also has a love for all animals. One of his favorite places to visit is the zoo. He wants to see each type of animal and learn about them. During his time at the Montessori preschool, his class had to practice a fire drill. Initially, Luke became extremely emotional during the drill, but once the children were allowed to return to the building, Luke ran to the rabbit's cage. He was so worried about what happened to the rabbit during the drill.

The biggest mistake we made in this process was waiting until after Luke was three before we got him the help he needed. We thought we had to wait. We thought we were following the norm. Now we realize he could have gotten help so much sooner.

Our advice to any other families starting down this road is to get as much help as you can as soon as you can. Don't wait! Also, follow your intuition instead of listening to others. People kept telling us that Luke was "all boy," and it distracted us from the real issue. We should have listened to our gut instinct from the beginning.

We would also encourage other families to learn as much as they can about their children's delays. Katie is an educator, so we felt we had a lot of information already. The problem was that this is not her specialty area, so we really didn't have all the information we needed. We are still learning, and we will be learning for a long time. Find a specialist, and ask lots of questions. Talk to other families that are going through the same challenges, and find out about the resources they have used. Always continue to learn. It will definitely help your child for the better.

# 3

# ASSESSMENTS AND CONFERENCES

It is essential that adults understand the developmental milestones of childhood so they can periodically use that information to assess the development of children. Every child, regardless of ability level and age, is moving through the progression of developmental milestones, and the important adults in that child's life need to constantly evaluate if the child appears to be on track. When a child is not developing at the same rate as similar-age peers, then it is critical to begin the early intervention process promptly. When a child receives early intervention at a young age, many developmental delays can be corrected quickly and may not have a long-term impact on the child.

## WHAT ARE ASSESSMENTS?

The typical definition of assessment would be an evaluation that determines whether or not something is working correctly or if a change needs to be made. When looking at early childhood education, the same general principle applies. The specialist evaluates the development of a young child to see if the child is growing and learning the way that is anticipated for a child of that age. It will also identify if there are areas that need to be addressed in order for the child to be developing at the appropriate rate. Although many specialists have worked with enough young children to understand what developmental skills to look for when working with a child, they normally use an assessment tool to collect the appropriate documentation about each area of the child's development.

The term "assessment tool" is used to represent a checklist or an evaluation that will look at each area of the child's development. On these tools, the child will get credit for the skills that he can complete successfully and independently. Once the specialist has been through each portion of the assessment tool, he or she will add up the total number of skills that the child completed to compile a final score. The tool typically gives the specialist a numeric range for children that are below target, within the target range, and above target for their developmental skills.

Since it is important to give each family correct information about the child and accurately assess the skills of each child, each assessment tool must be tested many times before it is considered reliable enough to use with children in a classroom or office setting. Although each company may use slightly different techniques to make sure their assessment tools are reliable, the same general principles apply.

Each company creates their assessment tool based on medical research about what skills a child has mastered at each significant age interval. Once the checklist or the evaluation questions are compiled, the company will ask for child volunteers to be assessed with the tool. The company's goal is to show that the vast majority fall in the middle of the assessment criteria or the category marked as "typically developing." There should be a much smaller population that rate in the categories that are below and above target. The scores of the children should look very similar to a bell curve.

Once the tool has been tested on a large population of children to determine the developmental norm for the age and abilities of the skills listed on the tool, then the tool is ready for use to show specialists if a child assessed with the tool is showing typical developmental milestones. Assessment tools are created for children within a certain age range, so if a company creates an assessment tool, they will have to make several tools to use for each developmental range.

There are several different types of assessment tools that are typically used with young children. The first tool is referred to as a screening tool. A screening tool is an abbreviated version of an assessment tool. It is much shorter than other assessment tools because it typically only has four or five questions to answer in each developmental category. For example, a screening tool for the motor skills of a child around twelve months of age may assess if the child can stand independently, can walk independently, and can use her fingers to pick up food and feed herself.

A screening tool is never used to make any type of diagnosis. Its primary purpose is to let the specialist know if any further evaluation needs to be done. If a child assesses well on the screening tool, there is typically not a need for further evaluation at that time. When a child scores poorly on a screening tool, that indicates to the specialist that more extensive evaluation should be conducted in order to assess the child's full skill set. Screening tools are typically used by doctors and classroom teachers on every child to get a general idea of development, so when a specialist asks to use a screening tool, it is not because he or she suspects a delay.

Another assessment tool frequently used with young children is a curriculum-based assessment, such as Teaching Strategies Gold. This tool is used by early childhood specialists and teachers to assess the curriculum skills that a child has mastered and which skills are emerging. If a preschool teacher is using a curriculum-based assessment to evaluate a child's gross motor skills, or large muscle skills, then the teacher would document which skills the child can already accomplish independently. The teacher will then look at the skills that the child can't complete independently, and he or she will use that information in the lesson plan process. New lessons will be planned in order to challenge the child and help the child master the next developmental milestone. Again, this type of assessment is used with all children, and using the tool does not mean that the specialist suspects a delay.

A young child may also be assessed with a diagnostic tool, such as the Battelle Developmental Inventory or the Bayley Scales of Infant Development. A diagnostic tool is much more extensive than a screening tool. It will look at every area of development, complete with subcategories in each of the areas. For example, in the area of gross motor development, a diagnostic tool may take an in-depth look at balance, coordination, flexibility, and strength. The tool may also incorporate a parent questionnaire to receive feedback from the family members to see what they notice about the child's development.

Along with numeric calculations for whether or not a child is capable of completing a skill independently, the specialist may need to write down observations about what he or she witnessed while observing or interacting with the child. There will be a specific way to calculate the results of the assessment tool, and the specialist must have specific training in order to score the tool accurately. The results of the assessment will be used to show if the child is developing in the typical range or if the child has a developmental delay in one or more areas. This type of tool is used for diagnosis, acquiring therapy or special education, and for creating a treatment plan that is specific to the needs of the child.

## WHO CAN ASSESS A CHILD?

Assessment tools are administered by specialists, but there is a wide range of specialists that are capable of administering these types of tools. Many assessment tools do not require a certain level of education to use the tool, but they do require professional development training to learn the specific steps the company has created for the tool that the specialist has selected. Many childcare providers and early childhood educators use screening tools and curriculum-based assessments as a regular part of their classrooms.

In order to use the tools, the teachers must be trained on how to complete the paperwork for the tool. The guidebook for the teachers will also include notes on how to determine if each skill was completed successfully, since some skills may be slightly subjective. For example, a screening tool may ask if a twelve-month-old child can walk independently. The program notes may further explain that the child must be able to take four or five steps in a row without falling down or holding onto something in order to be considered successful at walking independently.

Pediatricians also use screening tools on a regular basis. Many parents will fill out a parent questionnaire for the screening tool as they wait in the lobby for a well-child checkup. The screening tool will ask about developmental skills (e.g., if a child can sit up or babble), but it will also focus on health-related issues like hearing and vision. The American Academy of Pediatrics encourages every pediatrician to conduct these screenings at every well-child checkup.

The doctor will typically ask the parent about the developmental history of the child, ask about any concerns that parent may have, observe the child during the appointment, and document this information for a record of the child's overall health. When the pediatrician has concerns, he or she may ask for a follow-up appointment to see if the child grows out of a typical behavior or may ask for further evaluation. Children that have developmental delays are considered at medical risk, so the situation may be treated similarly to a child with a chronic illness. The pediatrician will typically encourage early treatment to avoid prolonged delays. Early treatment could be a referral to a specialty doctor, a special educator, or a therapist (like a speech pathologist or a physical therapist).

There are some assessment tools, particularly diagnostic assessment tools, that must be administered by a certified specialist. For example, if a child is being evaluated for a speech and language delay, then a certified speech pathologist or a diagnostic special educator will administer the evaluation. This happens for several reasons.

First, the area of development is so specific that it requires an expert in the field to conduct the evaluation properly and look for very particular details. Second, when the results of the assessment must be used to help a child qualify for health insurance supported services, such as speech therapy, then the health insurance industry needs verification that the assessment was conducted accurately. Finally, it can be very difficult for a child to go through a lengthy evaluation process with an adult the child may not know that well. The child may refuse to participate in the activities for the assessment or demonstrate very emotional behavior. Specialists that conduct evaluations as a primary job responsibility have developed skills to creating a safe and inviting environment for the children. Many children need a true diagnostic professional to get accurate assessment results.

## THE PURPOSE OF DEVELOPMENTAL ASSESSMENTS

Each type of assessment has its own purpose, but there are several overarching reasons that we use assessments as a tool to benefit all young children, regardless of ability level. First, assessments are a huge tool for teachers. All assessments give teachers (and early intervention specialists) a great deal of information about the child so they are able to create a classroom that benefits each individual student.

Assessments are a benefit for children that are above target, on target, and below target. If a child has already mastered all of the skills on which the teacher will be focusing during the school year, then the assessment can show the teacher where the student is excelling so the teacher can continue to challenge the child for the remainder of the school year. If the child is within the typical developmental range for his or her age group, then the teacher can confirm that the curriculum is meeting the student's needs. At the same time, a typically developing student can still be excelling in one specific area, so the assessment will help the teacher identify both the student's strengths and the student's challenges.

Assessment also creates a quality learning environment. When teachers understand the students' needs, they create classrooms that support those needs. When an entire school utilizes effective assessments, then the process of transitioning a student from one age classroom to another goes much smoother. The entire faculty at the school understands the developmental spectrum that the assessment tool is evaluating, so when a new child is moved to the classroom, there is a greater understanding about the child's developmental level.

When the entire school uses the same assessment system, then teachers can easily communicate information about students from one teacher to another as they move to the next learning environment. This type of assessment can also help the school with classroom placements by making sure a variety of students are placed in each classroom. This allows for each classroom to have positive role models, and it ensures that no teachers are overwhelmed, and thus can do their jobs to the best of their abilities.

Finally, assessments enable a strong parent-and-teacher communication system. Assessment information allows teachers to give families very specific and accurate information about their children's development, and assessment tools that incorporate parent questionnaires allow the parents to share information with the teacher that the teacher may not see in a classroom setting.

## HOW TEACHERS SHARE INFORMATION WITH FAMILIES

One of the primary responsibilities of an early childhood educator is to establish constant communication with the families of young children. This can be done in a wide variety of ways. Many early education programs do not have structured transportation, so the child's family must bring the child to school and pick the child up after school. The early educator needs to utilize this time and give the family information about the child's day, special interests, and special experiences that occurred during the school day.

Early educators also utilize a variety of technological methods of communicating with families. In past years, early childhood teachers may have printed a weekly newsletter to share information with families, but now many schools share their newsletters by email or the teacher posts a weekly blog to describe what is happening in the classroom that week. School websites and social media pages offer classroom reminders and show pictures of events that take place during the school day.

Personalized information is one method of communication that all families seem to value. Whether the teacher writes a handwritten card or sends an email, every family member enjoys hearing stories about what the child accomplishes during the school day and about new goals the child is achieving. Depending on the number of children in the classroom, the teacher may not be able to offer this personalized information frequently, but when it is possible, it is something most families truly cherish.

Despite the wide variety of communication methods offered to teachers, the parent-teacher conference is still the preferred method to share specific and confidential information about a child's development. Even though the teacher may see the family each day during drop-off and pick-up times, it is still better to set aside a special time to talk. When the teacher is in the classroom with the children, it will always be his or her primary responsibility to care for the children. That makes it difficult to have a conversation that lasts more than a couple of minutes.

Also, when parents are coming and going with their children, the classroom setting does not allow the teacher to offer a family a private environment to share personal information, whether that news is good news or development concerns. It is always best just to reserve a small amount of time outside of the classroom so the teacher and the parents have the opportunity to share information back and forth.

## THE PURPOSE OF A CONFERENCE

The primary purpose of a conference is for the child's family and the child's teacher to work as a team to create the best possible learning environment at school and at home. Conferences are a great time for parents and teachers to share information about how the child has made progress. Since families see the children in different settings, it is helpful for each to hear stories about how the child is growing and developing in different environments and around different people.

Conferences help families and teachers learn about the children's strengths and weaknesses. The parent is always the expert on the child. Even though a teacher may spend seven to eight hours a day with the child, the family sees the child every day throughout a long sequence of time. This gives the family insight that the teacher may not have. Also, the teacher sees the child in a structured, group setting with specific goals, so this is important information that the family does not always have. That is why it is so important for the family members and the teachers to work together.

Conferences also give families and teachers the opportunity to create a plan together to help children achieve their goals. These plans may be very simple. The teacher may offer tips that he or she is using in the classroom and suggest that the family uses the same strategies at home. The parent may be able to explain to the teacher about the best way to soothe the child, and the teacher can then plan to use that skill in the classroom.

It is important for families to keep in mind that conferences are not a negative communication tool. When many parents were young, con-ferences were used only when a child was in trouble or when something negative was happening in the classroom. That is no longer the model for early childhood education conferences. Now, teachers work to set up conferences with each family at least a couple of times a year in order to establish constant communication.

Conferences should not be reserved only for children that "have problems." Also, when teachers use conferences most effectively, they may schedule them at set points throughout the year to share progress, but they may also use conferences upon request. This could mean that the family can request a conference to talk about specific topics such as the transition to a new classroom or how to prepare for kindergarten. It can also mean that a teacher may request a conference to talk about changes in the classroom structure, to discuss a change in teaching staff, or to receive ideas from the family about how best to challenge the child during the school day.

Most parent-teacher conferences are typically scheduled for a set amount of time, such as thirty minutes, so the teacher can plan on being out of the classroom and giving the family his or her full attention during that time period. The conference may also include other school staff at the request of the teacher or the family. An administrator may be asked by the family or by the teacher to attend to discuss a school policy or to help problem-solve solutions that the teacher may not be able to resolve alone.

During a transition conference, the current teacher and the new teacher may both be present to help discuss the differences in the two classrooms. If a child receives support services, such as early intervention, the family and the teacher may invite the specialist to the conference in order to receive the specialist's expert opinion.

Before the conference, it can be very helpful for the family members to write down all the questions they have for the teacher in advance. It is easy to get off track during a conference while the teacher is sharing great stories about the child. A typical list of questions may include a child's schedule during the school day, whom the child chooses to play with during school, and what his or her favorite classroom activities are. This is also a great time for parents to list any concerns so they remember to ask the teacher how certain situations are handled or if it is possible to make any changes.

Families may want to plan on bringing a paper and pen along to most conferences because teachers will plan on sharing important information such as a child's developmental progress, strengths and weaknesses, and resources that may help the child to grow and develop further. Many teachers will use the conference time to share the results of screenings and curriculum-based assessments. The teacher may also share information about the child's behavior during classroom time, how he or she handles changes in the daily schedule, and any possible concerns with which the teacher may need support from the family members to resolve. The most important part of a parent-teacher conference is for teachers and parents to use the time together as a dialogue to share information and find ways to benefit the child.

# STORY 3: SOPHIA

## Told by Sophia's Mother, Jennifer

From the time that Sophia was a baby, she was so happy. One of the first things I remember about her was her sweet smile. She was such a content baby. Compared to her older brother, she had a very relaxed temperament. When I held my baby girl in my arms and watched her smile at me, I had visions of ballet recitals with her little pink tutu. It was so exciting to be the mother of this precious little girl.

Sophia was not as active as her brother had been as an infant, but everyone told me that boys just have more energy. For a while that seemed like a logical explanation. I started to be a little skeptical of that logic when Sophia did not begin to crawl until she was eleven months old. At first, I just thought she was on her own timetable, but by eighteen months, the differences in her and other children were far more noticeable. Sophia was still not walking, and she could speak very few words. The words she could speak were only recognizable to my husband and me. My mother was also starting to notice the development gap between Sophia and other children her age.

At this point, we thought it would be helpful to get an evaluation from a specialist to see if there was a diagnosable problem. We contacted First Steps, our state's early intervention program, and set up an evaluation. The week of the scheduled evaluation Sophia began taking her first few steps, so she no longer met the qualifications to receive early intervention. At that moment, I thought everything was fine. She started off developing a little bit slower than her friends, but now she had caught up and we were back on track.

It was around that same time period that Sophia began developing very strong stranger anxiety. Since I did not work outside of the home, I thought this might be normal since she spent so much time with me each day. I tried to make sure that I left her with other adults in the church nursery and other family members, but that didn't seem to lessen her separation anxiety. Frequently she cried the entire time that she was in the nursery at church, and none of the volunteers were able to soothe her even though she saw them every week.

Even though I was working hard at convincing myself that Sophia was fine, I watched and saw how the development gap between her and her peers continued to grow. Her vocabulary was not growing. She seemed oddly clumsy, like she couldn't get her arms and legs to move in the way that she anticipated. I continued to worry and began asking my friends what they thought.

By the time Sophia was two years old, one of my friends suggested that it was time for another speech evaluation. She worked in the field of early childhood education, and she said that typically children significantly increase their vocabulary between the age of eighteen months and two years of age. Since Sophia had not met this milestone, it would be beneficial to have a reevaluation. We set up another evaluation with First Steps, and this time Sophia qualified for speech therapy.

Sophia began receiving weekly speech therapy. Even though she was making small amounts of progress, it seemed she was falling further and further behind. I tried to compare her development to what I remember my son doing, and it did not seem similar at all. The speech pathologist told me she believed Sophia's symptoms seemed like speech apraxia.

Like any modern parent, I began to do my internet research, and the more I read, the more worried I became. I instantly started to focus on the worst-case scenario in each story and article I read. What if Sophia had autism? The speech pathologist and the pediatrician both told me they did not believe that Sophia had autism because she was extremely social. Sophia loved to smile and laugh with our family, and she was making eye contact when she tried to communicate with us.

Despite his assurances that Sophia only had a speech delay, the pediatrician referred us to Cincinnati Children's Hospital for an evaluation with a neurology specialist when Sophia was two and a half years old. The specialist told us he saw no neurological problems at this time, but I still did not feel we were getting to the root of the problem.

Around this same time, lots of things seemed to be changing in our life. We decided to go visit a preschool that specifically focused on helping children with speech and language delays. The preschool also had speech pathologists on staff that partnered with the preschool teachers to help the children receive the best possible care. The speech pathologist we were working with also noticed that Sophia was having significant issues with motor planning. She recommended that Sophia begin occupational therapy to work on her motor delays.

Currently, Sophia receives speech pathology twice a week in her preschool setting, and she sees a private occupational therapist once a week. They are treating her for speech apraxia, delays in motor planning, and sensory processing dysfunction. We have had a long journey to find the best combination of therapy for Sophia.

Our first pediatrician constantly assured me that everything would work out fine for Sophia, but he did not help me take action to get her the support services she needed. I really wanted a doctor for her who would listen to my concerns and validate them. We switched pediatricians, and it was one of the best decisions my husband and I have made for her care.

Our new doctor affirmed our concerns. He agreed with our choice of therapists, and he provided us with a referral to a developmental pediatrician (which seemed to be a more appropriate specialist for the delays with which Sophia is struggling).

When Sophia turned three, we had an official diagnosis completed with the public school system. The evaluation showed delays in language, motor, and adaptive skills. They also had some concerns about her social and emotional skills, but that was mainly due to her lack of language skills. Sophia's cognitive skills are exactly where they should be for a child her age. She can understand what others are saying. She knows all of her colors, and she can easily identify objects when you ask her questions like, "Where is the apple?" Although it is slightly delayed, she enjoys pretend play. She loves to rock her baby dolls, and she is now copying activities that she sees other people do (like talking on a cell phone).

One of the hardest things for me to deal with regarding Sophia's delays is that there is no specific diagnosis. If her condition had a name, it would be easier to explain to others and to have a specific prognosis. The therapists keep telling me that this combination of delays is something they see frequently, but I just want to have one term that I can use to explain to others what is going on so they can understand more easily.

One of the things I have struggled with throughout the process of diagnosis and treatment is a constant fear that something worse is coming. What if this is only the beginning of a much scarier path or diagnosis? Sophia is making progress, but it is hard not to worry about her. That is just what parents do. People have been telling me over and over that "she will be fine." Initially I clung to that, but now I have realized that isn't enough.

Every family that goes through this process has to find a way to deal with all the emotions that you struggle with each day. I had to stop hoping for things to go back to "normal." For me, I have had to rely on my faith in God. That is the only thing that has brought comfort.

Day-to-day life has been much different than I thought it would be. I envisioned that Sophia's life would be very similar to my older son's, but I just can't compare the two anymore. They are completely different children. Every day I go through a wide range of emotions. Some days I feel sorry for myself that my little girl is nothing like my friends' children. On days when Sophia conquers a major milestone, I am on top of the world!

I continue to convince myself that it does not matter what other people think of my child or how my family is dealing with her care and treatment. My husband has a talent for giving me a reasonable perspective on the situation. He does not worry about the possibilities the way I do, and he frequently reminds me that people are not analyzing our situation the way I imagine they are.

I quit my professional career when my children were born so I could stay at home with them. It seems odd now that Sophia had to start preschool so much younger than I anticipated. At the same time, I am thankful that I have the time to take her to therapy and learn from the therapists. That seems like a part-time job on its own sometimes. I am also shocked by the cost of the doctor's appointments and the therapy visits. I am so thankful that we have been able to provide all of these things for Sophia, but they do require us to make sacrifices at times.

Our whole family and several close friends have been extremely supportive during all of Sophia's challenges. They have been our "safe place" when I have worried about how the rest of the world has viewed my daughter and her delays. Our church has also been a source of great support. Ever since Sophia's initial stranger anxiety reached its peak at eighteen months, the church staff and volunteers have worked very hard to understand why Sophia is struggling and how they can support her. As much as I have loved the comfort that my friends and family have provided us, I have also needed some outside support.

Before Sophia's evaluation and therapy started, I had never really dealt with a lot of grief in my life. I have lost grandparents and had typical disappointments, but Sophia's situation affected me more than anything I have ever experienced. I typically thought about those little ballet shoes that I thought my daughter would wear for her first dance recital, and it seems like those dreams have died. I had to seek the help of a counselor to learn how to deal with this grief. I am trying to realize that even though the life I had planned for her may not occur, it does not mean that she won't have a wonderful life. Again, I continue to cling to my faith to deal with this loss, and I am so grateful for a husband who tries to steer me away from focusing on the worst-case scenario.

Even though Sophia does have several delays, there are so many wonderful things about her that I wish the rest of the world knew about! She loves to laugh. The sound of her laugh is one of the sweetest sounds I can imagine. She loves her brother, and even though he is only seven years old, he is a master at interacting with her. They chase each other around the house, and they love to play games with one another. Sophia has the gentlest temperament. She is sweet and kind. She is also very smart. I think that others don't anticipate that since she can't talk to them, but if they learn how to communicate with her, they are often shocked at what she knows. I also wish everyone knew how much Sophia enjoys interacting with others. She loves people!

If I could give advice to other parents who are worried about their children having a delay, the first thing I would say is get as much intervention as you can as early as you can. The sooner you start this process, the sooner you will see improvement. I wish I had listened to my gut instinct when I first thought Sophia was having problems instead of letting First Steps deter me. It won't hurt your children to get therapy if they are on the borderline of needing that support, and you don't want to have regrets later on for not starting sooner.

I would also tell parents that it helps to talk to others about what you are going through. You need all the support you can get. Don't blame yourself for what your children are going through. The most important thing to focus on is how you can help them now, not what you could have done differently.

Finally, I encourage every family to find the way that helps you to cope with the situation so you can be the most benefit to your children. Find a support group. Go to a counselor. Get involved in your church. Find a way to take care of yourself so you can take care of your children. The journey is challenging, but it is worth it.

# 4

# REFERRALS AND EVALUATIONS

**O**nce an adult (parent, teacher, pediatrician, etc.) has identified a need for further assessment of the child's development, there is a structured process that begins in order to meet the needs of the child and the family. The need could have been identified by an assessment tool used by a pediatrician or a teacher, but the need can also be identified by parent request.

Regardless of how the need was brought to light, there are several steps that can be taken before an actual referral is placed for a child to be formally evaluated. During the pre-referral period, the intervention process is called response to intervention (RTI). If the child is still showing delays after the RTI process—with parent permission—a formal referral will be made. The referral is the request for formal evaluation and diagnosis.

A team of specialists will complete the full evaluation over all the developmental areas to see where the child's delays are and if they are severe enough to qualify for special education services. Once the evaluation is complete, the team will reassemble with the family to explain the evaluation results.

## BEFORE A REFERRAL

Before a referral, it is important for the specialists involved to identify the developmental needs of the child and find an alternative education plan and activities that may help to stimulate the student's growth and development. There is a team of specialists that work together to create these ideas and challenge the student. The team is typically comprised of the primary teacher, the family or guardians, any necessary medical professionals, an administrator, and any other adult that is an integral part of the child's education (such as an early intervention therapist).

The primary teacher (or the developmental interventionist, if the child is seen on home visits) will give the team a summary of the child's developmental history and explain some of the difficulties that he or she has seen in the classroom setting. Once the team has the child's history, they can begin to brainstorm ideas and activities that can assist the child in the classroom.

At one point, students could only qualify for special education if they had a low IQ or a medically diagnosed condition that impaired their learning. This meant that many children with a delay in only one or two developmental areas could easily slip through the cracks of the system and not receive the support services they needed. In 2004, after the Individuals with Disabilities Education Act was updated, many states moved to a formal pre-referral process called RTI. The RTI system was used to create a fluid process that offers more support to students who have more involved needs.

RTI has a three-tier system to provide the amount of support that each student needs, and it involves using classroom and educational strategies that are evidence based and have research to support the fact that they are successful at assisting students with developmental delays. When a student participates in RTI, the team of specialists frequently monitors the child's progress to see if he or she is responding to the techniques being used and if new techniques need to be added. The specialists also collect data throughout the RTI process to track advances and instructional goals.

The three-tier system offers several different levels of support. Tier 1 focuses on using a high-quality general education curriculum with more individual support to meet the same common goals of the majority of students in the classroom setting. This involves the course content as well as behavior management strategies. The vast majority of students will respond positively to these types of intentional changes that still focus on the standard curriculum. Tier 2 utilizes smaller group instruction with some remediation of the standard class curriculum. If students do not show growth during this phase of RTI, they will move to the final tier. Tier 3 is the most intense level of RTI, and it uses specifically individualized interventions that may be more intensive or time involved.

The idea of the RTI system is to increase the child's mastery of the skills that teachers are demonstrating in the classroom. The first level of the RTI system allows the child to learn about the skill in the classroom with all of his or her peers, with the teacher only making small modifications. If the child still can't achieve mastery, the teacher or special educator will attempt to reteach the skill in a small-group setting with a little more intentionality.

Finally, if the child still has difficulty with mastery, the lesson is individualized, and the teacher works one-on-one with the child in order to help the child be successful. The child's support becomes more intentional and allows the child more time to achieve mastery. Despite increased support, if the child is still struggling with mastering a skill, then he or she may have an undiagnosed developmental delay.

Whether the school uses a pre-referral procedure or whether the school specifically uses the RTI procedure, the process should still look very similar. The purpose of this process is to find methods to help the student be successful in the classroom without having to enter special education. If the student does not show improvement (or only limited improvement) with the three different levels of RTI, then the team will refer the student for formal assessment to determine if he or she is eligible for special education.

When parents are considering whether or not they want their child to go through a formal evaluation process, it is important to remember that the teacher has already tried different types of strategies to help the child learn. The RTI process will look very different in a preschool than it does in an elementary school. The elementary school is going to focus on academic skills. However, a toddler or preschool classroom may be making adaptations to help a young child speak, toilet train, or play cooperatively with other children. The goals of RTI will be based on the child's age and developmental milestones.

## WHAT IS A REFERRAL?

A referral is the formal process that occurs when an adult requests further evaluation of a young child. When a child is under the age of three, the referral will typically be placed with the state's early intervention program that serves children from birth to three years of age. When the child is three years of age and older, the referral will be routed through the public school system.

Some families may opt not to use the public school system and have the child evaluated through a private therapy practice to see if the child qualifies for support services like occupational therapy or speech therapy through health insurance. This would be at the discretion and cost of the family. The public school system will provide the evaluation and create a plan for intervention for any child over the age of three, even if the child does not enroll in the public school classroom.

Whenever the state's early intervention program or public school system receives a request for a referral, the family is notified in writing immediately and asked to attend the pre-referral meeting. The pre-referral meeting occurs for the participants to discuss the reason for the referral, to explain the evaluation process, and to decide what areas of the child's development need to be evaluated. The parents must receive a copy of the rights of the child and family that are associated with the special education process. The family will need to review that information (with the team's support) because the family will have to sign a consent form for the evaluation process before it can begin. Without parent consent, the evaluation process cannot proceed.

The pre-referral team will ask the family for a lot of information before beginning the evaluation. The more information the family can offer, the better informed the specialist will be for the evaluation process. The team will need a full medical history and information about any medical diagnosis that the child already has. The parents will need to provide documentation from the physicians along with contact information for any of the doctors that the child is currently seeing. The signed parent consent for the evaluation gives the team permission to obtain these documents from the doctor and for the doctor to communicate openly with the team.

The family will also be asked to fill out a history of the child's developmental milestones. This will include providing information about when the child achieved skills such as crawling, walking, talking, and other major milestones. Families can document this information prior to the pre-referral meeting to save time for the evaluation team.

The family is also encouraged to share any other information they find important about their child. This can include what the child does and doesn't like, fears, and what motivates the child. The parents may want to provide documentation of the concerns they have regarding the child's development and situations that have worried the family. The family can share information from past teachers and any other documentation that could help the committee.

## WHO MAKES REFERRALS?

Several different adults can make a referral. First, it is important to know that the family always has a right to make the referral, even without supporting documentation of a specialist in the field. This is the same for early intervention services and public school special education. The parent knows the child best, and if the parent has concerns about the child's development, there is usually a strong reason.

School personnel also have the ability to initiate a referral, which can be general education teachers, special education teachers, counselors, or an administrator. Any other person involved in the care and education of the child can also initiate a referral. This is a broad category, but it can include physicians, therapists, childcare providers, foster parents, and other adults who are in some way responsible for the child. Although the referral can be initiated by several different individuals, the process cannot advance without the consent of the parents or guardians of the child.

## WHAT IS AN EVALUATION?

An evaluation is one of the early steps in the process to obtain special education services for a young child. The purpose of the evaluation is to address several important questions:

- Does the child need special education support in order to be successful?
- What areas of development specifically need additional support?
- What types of services and special education supports will the child need in order to advance developmentally?

In order to answer these questions, a multidisciplinary team will be assembled to evaluate the child. The law requires the child to have a full evaluation that is based on the individual needs of the child. This means that a full assessment of the child's development will take place, but additional specialized assessments may be utilized to look at individualized areas of need. For example, if the pre-referral meeting showed concerns regarding the child's speech and language skills and the child's response to stress, then the multidisciplinary team will most likely include a speech and language pathologist and a child psychologist or counselor to complete specific evaluations.

There can also be vision and hearing screenings as a part of the evaluation process. The team can also include a diagnostician, the general education teacher (or developmental interventionist for a child in a home visiting program), the special education teacher, necessary medical specialists, and any therapists or service providers that support the child. The family is always invited to participate on the child's team. The team will use both diagnostic assessment tools and observations to assess the child.

When a child under the age of eight is evaluated, the team is only identifying whether or not the child has a developmental delay in one or more of the developmental areas. Their goal is not to offer a specific diagnosis. When a child is over eight years old, it is common for a diagnosis like a learning disability to appear in the evaluation results. The exception to the rule with young children is if a child already has a specific medical diagnosis like cerebral palsy or Down syndrome. If the child is already diagnosed with this type of chronic condition, then it will be included in the evaluation documentation.

Each member of the evaluation team must be certified in his field and have previous experience with evaluating children. The team members will do their portion of the evaluation and then submit their reports to the team leader or committee chair. The team leader will summarize the evaluation report and create a report to summarize the outcomes of the evaluation. The school district is required to complete the evaluation within sixty working days of the referral date. It is also essential that the evaluation be conducted in the child's primary language and that the child is evaluated in the natural environment.

The school will schedule the child's evaluation, but it is essential that the time and place of the evaluation work for the family. The school will be working to complete the evaluation process quickly; however, the family has the right to speak up and ask for different arrangements. The family also needs to speak up if the assessment is not in the child's native language. If the family speaks a different language at home, it is essential for the parents to let the school know which language is preferred for the evaluation.

Even if a doctor diagnosed the child with a specific medical evaluation, it is still essential for the child to go through the evaluation process to see if she qualifies for special education services. Many different medical conditions have a spectrum of symptoms, so some health conditions that children have may not be serious enough to need additional special education support. Even children with more significant medical needs will need to go through the evaluation process to gauge the extent of the special education support they will need.

The evaluation summary is invaluable to the professional team because it gives a detailed description including every area of the child's development. When a child does qualify for special education services, this summary is the information that will help the teachers and specialists set achievable goals for the child. It will also establish which types of supports need to be provided for the child to have the best possible learning experiences.

## WHAT DO EVALUATION RESULTS MEAN?

After the evaluation summary is created, the family and the evaluation team meet to review the results and how they will affect the child's education. The evaluation results meeting must happen within forty-five school days of the day that the parent or guardian signed permission for the evaluation to take place according to the Individuals with Disabilities Education Act. After the team leader shares the results of the evaluation, every member of the evaluation team will sign the summary report to show if he or she approves or disapproves of the evaluation summary. If a member of the team disagrees with the summary report, then he or she can submit a written report listing his or her objections and explaining why the report (or a portion of the report) should be reconsidered. At the conclusion of the meeting, the parents or guardians will be sent written notification to tell them if the child qualifies for special education services.

If the child qualifies for special education services, the family will be invited to attend a meeting to create the child's Individualized Education Program (IEP). If the child is under the age of three, the team will create an Individualized Family Service Plan (IFSP) where the family's role is slightly more involved than in the IEP. The Individuals with Disabilities Education Act also states that the IEP meeting must take place within thirty calendar days of determination that the student qualifies for special education services.

The IEP meeting is a meeting to discuss the results of the child's evaluation, the child's developmental needs, and the supports the child may need in order to be successful in the natural environment. The team then creates an individualized plan for the child's education. The plan includes the child's placement, support services, and how the child will receive services (the environment, frequency, etc.). The IEP and the IFSP are legal documents that guarantee the child the special education supports he or she is offered at the IEP meeting.

It is also important for families to remember that not every child struggling with development will qualify for an IEP or an IFSP. Sometimes there is a developmental delay, but it is not significant enough for the school or the early intervention agency to offer an individualized plan. These children might still need additional support, but the state programs will not cover the cost of the services.

Many children do not qualify for state programs, but their evaluation will still allow their health insurance company to approve the child for supports like occupational therapy or speech therapy. In this situation, it is also essential that the parents stay in communication with the child's teachers or pediatrician to create a plan to monitor the delay. If the child begins to fall further below essential developmental milestones, it may be time to request a reevaluation.

# WHAT OPTIONS DO YOU HAVE AFTER THE EVALUATION?

When the family receives the results of the evaluation, the family members have several things to consider. First, if a child qualifies for special education services, then the parents or guardians need to decide if they want to accept those services. The family is not required to accept services, and the school district can't offer special education services without parent permission. It is important for the family to remember that any special education services offered can advance the child's current level of development, and when services begin early in life, it is possible the child will surpass the need for continued special education supports. Despite the benefits, it is always the family's decision whether to accept or deny special education services.

If the results show the child did not qualify for special education services, the family members must decide if they believe the results of the evaluation are accurate. If they believe the results are accurate and the child's developmental delay was just not significant enough to qualify for special education, the family does have the option to pursue therapy at the cost of the family or with the help of medical insurance.

If the family does not agree with the results of the evaluation, they must take a different approach. If a child does not qualify for special education and the family disagrees with that decision, the family has the right to have an independent educational evaluation (IEE). This is an evaluation done by a qualified professional who does not work for the public school system or the early intervention program.

If the family asks for an IEE, the school district is required to provide the family with information about qualified specialists who could do this type of evaluation. The family must remember that independent educational evaluation specialists are often not free, and the school district is usually not obligated to cover the cost of this service. The family can petition for the service to be paid, but they may not have enough documentation to prove that the school district should provide this service. If the IEE evaluation contradicts the information from the school district's evaluation, the family can petition for the school district to reevaluate and provide the child with special education.

# STORY 4: ERICA

## Told by Tammy, Erica's Mother

**M**y daughter Erica is twenty years old, but her story actually begins before she was born. Erica was a honeymoon baby. My husband and I found out we were pregnant with her about two months after we were married. At that point we were still trying to blend two different families together. I had been the single mother of three children, and our family was now adding Connor, my new husband. The children were still getting to know what it was like to live with him and for him to be a part of our family when we found out I was pregnant.

During one of my prenatal exams, the doctor had concerns. We were sent to a perinatal specialist, where we found out our baby had tested positive for Down syndrome. When I look back, I feel that we received very little information about the diagnosis. The doctor told my husband and me that our baby would have Down syndrome, and then he told us that we still had a little bit of time to determine if we wanted to keep the pregnancy. We were left alone in a small room for what seemed like an eternity.

I know the hospital staff wanted us to consider the implications of both options: raising a child with a disability and terminating the pregnancy. Connor and I felt there was nothing to choose at this point. One of our other children could become disabled next week from a car accident or an illness. If that occurred, we would still love our child. There are no guarantees that a healthy baby will remain healthy. We knew we were meant to raise this baby, so our minds were already made up.

Once we left the doctor's office, I was on a mission to learn everything I could about Down syndrome. There was no internet then, so I was going to the public library searching for all of the information I could. I quickly learned not to read anything that was more than five years old. Past generations had viewed Down syndrome as a horrible disability with little hope of a child participating in typical activities. Many of the oldest writings encouraged institutionalizing a person with Down syndrome, or assumed the child would have a very short lifespan. Newer writing was definitely more positive, but there were still very troubling stories. As I read more and more about this chronic condition, I tried to share stories with my husband. He did not want to hear worst-case scenarios. He wanted to wait until Erica was born and see what needed to be done.

As I continued to read articles and books about what Down syndrome was, I felt more and more isolated. We lived in a pretty large town, but I did not know anyone who had a child with Down syndrome. Were there other families here that were going through the same thing? It seemed we were the only people who had ever dealt with this! How was I supposed to find someone to ask about this subject?

The library became so important to me because the doctors were not giving me information. Since the day of our diagnosis, the doctors acknowledged that she had Down syndrome, but we just didn't receive much information about it. I assumed that the doctors didn't know much about it either. At that time, we were working with the OB-GYN, the perinatalist, and a pediatric cardiologist. The pediatric cardiologist did tell us that the ultrasound showed a small hole in Erica's heart, but he also told us that this is not that unusual. For most children that are born with this type of defect, the heart heals itself over time. Instead of worrying about a heart murmur, I was focusing on what life would be like to raise a child with Down syndrome.

Before Erica was born, Connor and I made the decision not to tell Erica's siblings about her condition. We didn't want them just to know their sister as the baby with Down syndrome. We wanted them to get to know Erica. We wanted them to learn about what she liked, what she disliked, and what made her smile. Eventually, we would have to tell them about her diagnosis, but we didn't feel it was time for that yet.

When Erica was born, the reality of her diagnosis was worse than we had initially anticipated. Of course, we knew she had Down syndrome, but that was not all of her diagnosis. Instead of one small hole in her heart, Erica had three holes in her heart and a mitral value that was barely working. Her full diagnosis included Down syndrome and congenital heart failure. We would find out several years later that she also had bilateral hip dysplasia, but that was not diagnosed at birth.

The risk of infection was too high in the hospital, so they sent us home after three days. She was isolated from any type of illness and germs, so very few people were allowed to see her. Then after her first heart surgery, she was hospitalized for a full eight weeks. Connor and I stayed by her bedside whenever possible. There were times we were only allowed to sit in the waiting room, but we did everything we could to support her at all times. I was worried my other children would feel neglected during this time period, but when I talked to them about it, I reassured them that if they ever needed me this way, I would be at their bedsides just as I was at Erica's bed. They truly seemed to understand and never appeared to be frustrated.

The hospital did an excellent job of connecting us with the state's early intervention program during our stay there, but Erica was three months old before she was even well enough to interact with the therapists. It was a huge risk for her to interact with others because she could possibly have gotten sick and her heart may not have been able to sustain her. We were very isolated during those first few months.

Of course, our family (Connor, the three oldest children, and I) were all trying to work as a team to support one another, but it was very hard for anyone else to support us. Families from church tried to do things like drop off meals on the front porch, but they couldn't come in to visit.

Before Erica's birth, Connor and I both had jobs. After Erica was born, it became obvious that I would need to quit my job to stay home with her. There was not a childcare program that would support her health situation. We had to tube feed Erica every two hours. A feeding took up to forty-five minutes, and then we had to have her lie still for thirty minutes after the feeding. This was something that had to be done in the home.

Once therapy started, we had specialists that had to visit the home to evaluate her development and support her developmental goals. Since Erica had a qualifying condition like Down syndrome, we didn't have to wait through a lengthy evaluation process for services, as many children do. On the other hand, her fragile medical condition limited many other activities.

With a medically fragile child and three other children, it became more and more challenging to leave the house at all. We lost half of our income when I had to quit my job, so we stopped doing things like going out to eat dinner. It was essential to become frugal. We had private health insurance when Erica was born, but due to her lengthy hospital stay after her first heart surgery and all of her specialty care, we left the hospital with medical bills that totaled over $150,000. Of course, owing this amount of money is overwhelming. I was worried about paying it back, but the reality of Erica's health put everything into perspective. When you are worried about whether or not your child will be alive in a few months, it just seems ridiculous to stress over paying off hospital bills.

As a mother, there were plenty of things I was worrying about each day, but whether or not Erica would survive was always at the top of my list. I worried about my four other children. (My daughter Elizabeth was born when Erica was only twenty-two months old.) Was I spending enough time with them? How would all of this affect them? I was worried about the money. We just lost half of our income, and in only a few months we had accumulated a huge amount of hospital bills. I was still worried about my new marriage and our new blended family.

Even though these thoughts rolled around in my head quite a bit, I could see how Erica was bringing our family together. Everyone was working as a team to take care of her, including my other children. As a mother, this made me so overjoyed, even though I was dealing with many other emotions.

The finances were definitely a big part of my worries, and the hospital bills were at the top of that list. When Erica first came home from the hospital, I usually spent at least two hours a week on the phone with the health insurance company contesting their refusal to pay for something. I noticed when something was denied, it was usually because it was coded the wrong way in the doctor's office, and the insurance company was very particular about which codes they would pay for and which codes they denied.

Of course, Erica's medical bills did not stop when she came home from the hospital. They continued to accumulate with doctor's visits, therapies, and multiple surgeries over the years. As more medical bills added up, I continued to dedicate weekly time to calling the health insurance company, being transferred to the next department I needed to speak with, and appealing the claims that the insurance company denied.

After I had been fighting with our private health insurance company for a while, one of the doctors finally mentioned to me that Erica could qualify for Medicaid due to her disability. Not only would this take a great deal of financial pressure off of our family, but also Medicaid may make it easier for her to get certain services due to an official diagnosis of a disability.

At first this idea mortified me! I just could not believe I was going to go to the Cabinet for Health and Family Services and ask for government support. I had been the single mother of three children, and I had supported our family without any help. I felt as if accepting government support for Erica's medical care was a low point for me, but it wasn't possible for our family to continue with these expenses on our own.

After years of Erica receiving Medicaid, I don't have the same opinion. I came to realize that Medicaid is available for situations like our family's situation. Our daughter's medically fragile state encouraged us to reach out for this resource, even though the rest of our family was still using our private health insurance company. Most people that look down on someone for accepting support like Medicaid have no idea how overwhelming the financial obligations are. It is a situation you don't understand until you experience it yourself. Now, I am grateful for the support that we have, instead of feeling guilty or ashamed.

Aside from medical expenses, there were still a lot of bills to pay for with a family of seven people and only one job. Connor worked long hours to support us all so that I could give Erica the care she needed in our home. We still had groceries to buy. Erica needed high-calorie concentrated formula for her tube feedings. We still had normal household bills. Even with all of this happening, I was still more focused on my family being safe and healthy than all of the "what if" situations I could be stressing about. I just had the faith that we would always have groceries. I really began to distinguish (in my own mind) what was a top priority and what was not. My daughter's health was at the top of my priority list, and making late payments to the hospital was never going to be in the same category.

People will often ask me now how we got through these experiences, and the honest answer is that we got through them because we had to get through them. There was no choice. I had to care for my daughter. We had to live on one income. I had to care for all five of my children. You do it because you must.

We made a lot of sacrifices and gave up a lot of things that became luxuries in our new life. When I did have an opportunity to do something for myself, I took advantage of it without feeling guilty. One year for Mother's Day, the only thing I asked for was several hours for a nap. Since Erica had to be tube-fed every two hours, I rarely got a nap. Many people may not view a two- or three-hour nap as a gift, but it was amazing to have that time to myself.

Erica was two and a half years old before we realized how many families were in a similar situation to our own. One day the therapist asked me if we were going to the Buddy Walk that weekend. I had never heard of the Buddy Walk. She explained it was an annual event that was sponsored by the local Down syndrome society to create awareness about Down syndrome in the community. We decided to go that weekend.

It was amazing to find out there were other families in our community experiencing the same challenges we were. We learned about other resources available to us. This was the first time I had felt a part of a community since Erica was born. Erica was able to be a part of play groups with other children, and we knew families that we could go to with questions. We could ask other families if their children had been successful in public school or if we should try private school. We could ask families which doctors had the best bedside manner with their children. This made a huge difference! I knew that our city was too big for our Erica to be the only child with Down syndrome, but I didn't know where these other families were. We had finally found them! It was a huge encouragement.

As Erica approached the age of three, we had to determine what our next step was. Until that point, she had been receiving therapy in our home, but she was preparing to age out of the early intervention system in our state. Most children in our state went to public school preschool at age three if they had a diagnosed developmental delay. This meant that Erica would go to preschool for three hours a day and receive her therapy at school. Because Erica was medically fragile, I was really nervous about this transition.

Children who qualified for public school preschool could go to the preschool in their normal school district, if the district had a preschool program. My older children were already attending our local elementary school, and it was an amazing school. This gave me some reassurance, but I wanted to go and observe the classroom to see what it was like and if it would be a good fit for Erica. I contacted the school principal to see when I could observe the classroom, and I was told it wasn't possible for me to observe.

Our local public school was highly acclaimed, so many families had been petitioning the school to observe in the preschool classroom. The school decided to act in the best interest of the children, and the school's decision-making council made a policy that no one could observe in the classroom. When the principal told me this I was very confused. I told her, "I understand that you may want to limit outside visitors coming in and out of the classroom, but I am a potential parent. I need to observe the classroom to see if it is safe for my daughter." The principal said that school policy would not allow me to view the classroom, even as a potential parent.

I had already started to worry about many aspects of Erica starting school. Will she have friends? Since she is nonverbal, will she be able to convey her needs to her teachers? Will she stay healthy? I had never thought I would have to worry about whether or not I would be allowed to see the classroom. I would not send my daughter to a classroom that I was not allowed to see. Some aspects of public school truly support students with special needs, but this was definitely a negative policy.

When it appeared that public school preschool would not be an option for Erica, I began looking at private-pay preschool options. One of the schools I considered was a well-respected Montessori preschool in our area. I thought that a hands-on approach would better meet Erica's learning needs. The school was expensive, but if it was a good fit for her, then Connor and I agreed it would be worth it.

I went to the school to find out about enrollment and was blatantly told they would not be able to offer Erica a spot. The school said they just didn't have the staff or the ability to help her the way that she needed them to. I was standing in the office with my checkbook in my hand, preparing to give them money, and they were telling me no. This was a slap in the face. I had never considered that a school would not want to educate my daughter. I thought that as long as I was willing to pay for private education, the school would be willing to accept her.

Now I was faced with the reality that she would not be welcomed at every school. Of course, most private schools do not have the special education support that public schools offer because they are not legally obligated to do so. I know that many private school teachers are not trained on how to work with children that have the type of disabilities that Erica has. It was still shocking to stand there and realize that my daughter needed more help than they were willing to offer.

Despite our initial discouragement, we were able to find the perfect preschool program for Erica. Our local university had an early childhood education lab school that was able to serve children with disabilities. Erica attended that program until she was eligible for kindergarten, and then she moved to our neighborhood elementary school.

Public school was our first experience with an Individualized Education Program (IEP). Obviously we knew she would always need special education services, but we just weren't familiar with the bureaucracy and the paperwork involved in special education. At our very first special education meeting about Erica, I was given a copy of the parents' rights and the committee members asked me to review them and sign that I had been presented with the information.

The document was long, so I began to read. One of the committee members asked if I intended to read the entire document, and I told her I was going to read all of it before I signed off. She told me there was not enough time in the meeting for that. They had placed substitutes in the classroom for the teachers that were needed for the meeting, and those teachers needed to return to the classroom promptly. I responded by saying they would have to reschedule the meeting because I was going to read everything. They all seemed shocked. When we went home I asked Connor if they thought I was going to sign without reading. He said he assumed most people must do that or they wouldn't have looked so shocked.

As I sat at home reading the list of parent rights, I noticed it said the child has the right to be evaluated in the most comfortable environment. The school had told me that I needed to bring Erica in to their building for her evaluation. That was not where Erica felt most comfortable.

I told the committee I wanted her evaluated at home, and their initial reaction was, "We can't do that." I brought out my parent rights and told them they were required to do that. They did eventually do her evaluation in our home.

That was really my first lesson on advocating for my child in the public school system. After I took the time to read my parent rights and advocate for my daughter and me, the entire tone of the committee meetings changed. Instead of the committee telling me what I needed to do, it seemed we were all on equal footing from that point forward.

Still, I constantly had to ask the committee members to explain themselves. They were always using terms and acronyms I didn't understand. At first I asked the committee for a "cheat sheet" of acronyms and terms that would be used in the meetings. Once they gave me a list of the terminology, I still had a hard time understanding the conversation because they used the terms so quickly that I couldn't understand the context. I did have a textbook definition of what the "least restrictive environment" meant, but I still couldn't figure out how that applied to my daughter. I just continued to ask lots and lots of questions.

Overall, the IEP meetings we had in elementary school were really good, and I felt the committee wanted to work with us instead of tell us what to do. The transitions to middle and high school were much more complicated.

When we sat down with the IEP team members for Erica's high school experience, there was a very different tone to the meetings. Basically, the special educators that were going to work with Erica now had the overall goal that "we will keep her safe." This was not enough for me. I wanted her to learn how to use money. I wanted her to learn about how to be a productive member of society. I wanted her to be in collaborative classrooms for children with and without special needs.

The committee told me that the school's decision-making council did not allow collaborative classrooms. At that point, my husband decided it was time we got involved in school policy, and he ran for a seat on the board that made these decisions. He won and was able to sit on the board as a parent representative and give a voice to the families who needed special education services at the school.

I knew that my daughter wasn't going to be able to take calculus classes, but in many ways, I wanted the same things for her that most parents want. I wanted her to learn the skills to give back to the community, make a livable wage, and follow the law. The special education instructor at that time did not seem to believe that Erica could be a productive member of society, but I knew she could if she was taught. It may take her years to learn a skill that other children learn in days or weeks, but she will learn it.

By the time Erica was in high school, we had been having the same fight so often that Connor and I decided it would be in Erica's best interest to be homeschooled. With individual and repetitive instruction, Erica is now able to balance a checkbook, use the U-scan machine at the store, and add and subtract triple digit numbers. In a few years I believe she will be able to multiply and divide. I don't ever want her to stop learning because I know she can accomplish big goals.

Erica is also learning to be a part of the community. She folds bulletins at our church, volunteers at Meals on Wheels once a week, and participates in activities with our local Down syndrome association. One thing I know for sure about my daughter is that she has a definite purpose in this world. She was meant to be here and contribute to the world around her. She needs to be taught about those interactions, but she can rise to many challenges better than others anticipate. Her high school teachers did not seem to understand that.

There are many different options when you decide how to educate your child with special needs. Each family has to look at the situation that works best for them. We had both positive and negative experiences in public school, and as our family's needs changed, we had to change our education plan. You must pick the situation that works best for your family.

One tricky part about public school is that families can't ask for what they don't know exists. A great school or a great teacher will tell you about all of your options, but if you don't have those resources, you need to educate yourself. For example, when Erica was in elementary school, the school came to us and told us that our school did not have an FMD classroom. FMD stands for "functional mental disability," and an FMD classroom specializes in more significant disabilities. They told us Erica would need to go to an elementary school with an FMD room, instead of the classroom she was currently in. This meant we would have to separate her from her older siblings and a school that we were already comfortable with.

Just at the point when we were starting to lose hope, a teacher told us that we have the option to waive our right to the FMD classroom and keep her in her current classroom. I had no idea we could do that. I immediately signed the form and waived our right to move schools to the more specialized classroom. Not every family has someone there to tell them these tricks of the trade. That is one reason it is so important to educate yourself and ask others for help. Parents can't ask for something they don't know even exists.

Outside of school, we have been blessed with an amazing family. Erica has three older siblings and one younger sibling. All of her siblings do an excellent job of helping take care of her, and they have stepped in whenever we have needed them to do so. There has never been any resentment toward Erica. I have seen families where the other children do begin to envy the attention that a sibling receives or they get upset when their sibling with special needs inconveniences their lifestyle. My children truly love their sister, and I am grateful every day for that. It also gives me reassurance that if anything were to ever happen to my husband or me, Erica has four siblings who are able to step in and take care of her.

Although we didn't initially tell our children about Erica's diagnosis, Connor and I finally decided one day when Erica was two months old that we were going to tell her older siblings. It was a nice day outside. I sat Erica down on the bed and asked them what they thought of their little sister. "Do you love your little sister?" They told me that yes, of course they loved her. I asked them if they noticed anything special about her. I asked them about the shape of her eyes. My oldest daughter told me that Erica's eyes looked like that because she had Down syndrome. They looked at me as if they couldn't believe I didn't know this already.

My oldest daughter told me about a child at school with Down syndrome whom she frequently ate lunch with, even before Erica was born. I thought I had withheld information from them so they could get to know their sister without a label. My children had known the label the entire time, but it never affected their love for their sister. Then they asked if they could go outside to play, and that was end of what I thought was going to be a momentous conversation. Instead, they thought I was making a big deal out of nothing. It just reaffirms that I have wonderful children!

Outside of our family, it is harder for people to understand our family life. Our church is filled with compassionate people with great intentions, but it is still hard for them to understand the type of support that Erica needs to be included in regular activities. When you have an organization like a church, which runs primarily with volunteers, you know that most volunteers do not have experience working with children with significant disabilities.

When Erica was in first grade, it was time to switch to new Sunday school classrooms for the upcoming school year. We went into the new classroom, and the volunteer teacher looked at us and said, "I think you are in the wrong place." She apologized and rephrased her statement, but what she meant was that she didn't know how to work with my daughter.

I went to speak to our children's pastor because I was crushed by her statement. Everyone should be accepted at church. He agreed that I should be upset. He found an additional volunteer to help Erica be a part of the class. I appreciated his encouragement and management of the situation, but I still knew the teacher was overwhelmed just by seeing my daughter arrive on Sunday morning.

We have also had the opportunity to work with volunteers who I truly believe have been a gift from God. When Erica was in middle school, the other children her age were going through the confirmation process. She wasn't able to comprehend all of the topics they were covering, but we still wanted her to get to participate. Erica met with the whole group at the beginning of each session, but when the students broke into small groups each week, an amazing volunteer, who had been a speech and language pathologist by trade, offered to work with Erica individually to make her confirmation lessons more meaningful. I completely believe that most of Erica's understanding about God comes from those individual lessons with this amazing volunteer who stepped in to fill a very specific need, and I will appreciate that every day of my life. I wish everyone understood my daughter that way.

People are often anxious around Erica. She is very small in stature, so they assume she is still very young. Unfortunately, they often talk to her that way too. When Erica was in her teens, people frequently spoke to her as if she was in preschool. Then they would be shocked to learn her true age.

I don't get mad about this anymore. I just want people to know that Erica is capable of so many things! She can learn. She can benefit those around her. She has been put on this earth for a purpose. It makes me crazy when people tell me that our main objective should be to keep her safe. Her purpose on this earth is not to spend all day sitting on a couch. She is a lifelong learner, like many other adults. She is always improving her knowledge and her skills. If she can have a full conversation at thirty years old, it won't be amazing. It will be a product of her hard work and determination. It is because she is capable.

Now that Erica is in her twenties, our situation in life has changed somewhat. I am not only a mother now; I am a grandmother. Even though four children have grown up, I will never be an empty-nester. I have friends who are traveling and preparing to retire. Connor and I will always have a child at home to take care of, but I work hard to make sure I never resent that.

It sounds so harsh to think you would resent your child. Of course, I love Erica more than you can imagine, but if you start to think about what you "don't have" or what you "should have" it is easy to let resentment sneak in to your mindset. Now I am starting to think about how I will continue to parent Erica for the next thirty years. How will I care for Erica when she is fifty and I am eighty? I have to worry about my health more than many other parents, because my goal is to outlive my child. That is the prayer that no family would every utter, but when you have a child with significant special needs, you just want to live at least one day longer than she will. You want to be there every day to take care of her.

I am lucky that our family is so close and that her siblings will always be willing to step in when I need them to help. I know that as a family we get frustrated with one another at times, but I truly believe Erica has helped us all learn perspective. We are more focused on what is important, and we value our family a great deal.

After everything I have learned so far, I want other families to know that it is essential to educate yourselves. Learn everything you can about your child's disability. Talk to everyone you can and find out everything you can possibly comprehend. Learn about special education so you can demand the best possible education for your child. Learn how to advocate for your child, and never be embarrassed to fight for what he or she needs. Start developing a community of support when your child is young. If you get involved in local support groups, Special Olympics, and other community agencies that bring families together, the people you meet can be the best resources you will have throughout your child's life. These relationships and your knowledge about your child's health and school are your greatest assets.

# 5

# THE BURDEN ON THE FAMILY

When parents first learn they are expecting a child, so many emotions accompany this knowledge. Before a new baby is even born, the family begins to dream of what the child's life will be like. They dream about seeing the child accomplishing major milestones from learning to walk all the way to graduating from college or getting married. The father of a little girl may dream of the secrets they will share, or the mother of a little boy may dream about attending little league games. All parents want their children to be successful, intelligent, kind, happy, and healthy.

Many parents even dream that their children will surpass their own skills and dreams. Family members may think about these dreams throughout the pregnancy, or even years before the child is conceived. When the family learns that the child has a developmental delay (whether they learn before the child is born or as the child grows and develops), these dreams can come to an abrupt halt.

## WHAT IS CHRONIC SORROW?

Suddenly the family is focused on the loss of the perfect life they had planned for the child. Although the child is not lost, the family experiences a sense of mourning. They begin to mourn the loss of the child they planned for, not the child they have. This is frequently called chronic sorrow. Chronic sorrow is a reoccurring and overwhelming sensation of grief that parents and caregivers may experience throughout the life of the child.

Families of children with special needs and chronic health conditions frequently experience this type of profound sadness. It is a normal reaction to how the mind deals with such a serious life event, and it is a continuous process that helps the family member deal with a living loss. The parent or caregiver is battling with the realization of "what is" compared to what they believe "should be."

The family members will experience time periods of immense sadness, but they will also experience times of contentment or even joy. Unfortunately, medical or developmental setbacks can trigger new surges of chronic sorrow. Some of the most common reasons for family members to experience chronic sorrow include the following:

- A health crisis
- Exhaustion or unending caregiving
- Feelings of loss and guilt
- Further delays in development
- Comparing the child to same-age peers or typically developing siblings

Every parent and caregiver experiences a wide range of emotions when raising children. It is a hard job that has no established set of rules and directions. This means that every parent has periods of joy and sadness. The difference between the typical stressors of parenthood and chronic sorrow is that the latter is typically caused by disabilities, injuries, or chronic health conditions. The most common causes of chronic sorrow include the following:

- Developmental delays
- Down syndrome
- Epilepsy
- Neural tube defects
- Sickle cell anemia
- Diabetes
- Childhood cancer
- Mental health disorders

## STAGES OF GRIEF

Since chronic sorrow involves the family dealing with the loss of the life they had planned for the child, it is essential for families to understand what the grieving process looks like. When someone experiences a significant loss (typically the death of a loved one, but other losses apply as well), he or she will move through five distinct stages of emotions:

1. Denial and isolation
2. Anger
3. Bargaining
4. Depression
5. Acceptance

### Denial and Isolation

When a family enters the first stage of grief—denial and isolation—the typical response is to deny that anything is wrong with the child. Parents may attend a conference with the teacher and refuse to let the teacher proceed with a referral or evaluation because they believe the child is fine. Other parents may ask the doctor to redo multiple medical tests because they find it impossible that the child has a medical condition no one else in the family has ever had.

When parents are immersed in this level of denial, they will tend to isolate themselves from others so that no one can prove them wrong. It is easier to deny that your child has a delay if you do not spend time with your child or with other children the same age. It is easier to deny that the doctor may be accurate if you do not go back to that doctor or do not discuss the diagnosis with anyone else.

Even when parents try to deal with the situation rationally and factually, they may still find themselves frequently saying, "This can't really be happening." The doctor, the teacher, or a close friend may have to wait to present the information to the parents at a later time when they have had time to adjust to the news of the child's disability or illness. Some professionals may choose to only introduce the information initially so that the parents are not overwhelmed. They are trusting that another professional will bring the information to the family again and that the parents will be more prepared to accept the information the second time it is introduced.

## Anger

Once the family is willing to admit that the child does have a delay, a disability, or a chronic condition, family members typically move to the second stage of grief, anger. During the stage of anger, the family is usually looking for someone to blame for the child's situation. Parents may get angry with the doctor for providing poor health care. The family could get angry with the teacher for not helping the child to advance. Frequently, parents are mad at each other or themselves for contributing to the situation.

Finally, many families are mad at the universe or at their god. They just want to be mad at someone for what is happening to their children. Many caregivers and parents eventually get tired of being angry and move beyond this stage of grief. However, as it is with any stage of grief, there are some individuals who get stuck in anger and cannot move past it.

## Bargaining

The third stage of grief is bargaining. This is an internal monologue where the parent is continuously trying to make a deal with the universe or with God. "If I can be a good person for the rest of my life, can you please heal my child?" or, "If I will take my child to therapy and do everything the doctor asks, will you please fix my child?" The family continuously creates these deals, but when miracles do not occur, they move deeper and deeper into profound sadness.

## Depression

Failed bargains lead to the fourth stage of grief, depression. Most people understand the implications of depression, but in the framework of chronic sorrow, it has two different implications. The first type of depression is more practical. The family is worried about the child. They are trying to cope and deal with regular setbacks while still functioning in day-to-day life.

The second type of depression is much more subtle but extremely profound. This is when the family just begins to give up. They are no longer fighting to help the child or fighting to lead a normal life. Instead, they may feel like giving up on life. Many families may not have looked for professional help during the first few stages of grief, but depression begins to affect many different areas of a person's life. Parents may look for outside help from a counselor, a support group, or a church leader. Depression is significant enough that the family member will need help in order to move past this stage.

## Acceptance

The final stage of grief is acceptance. Many people experiencing grief never evolve to the stage of acceptance. Others may reach acceptance at one point but then experience a trigger that sends them back to the beginning stages of grief. This cycle can be continuous and ever changing. It is essential for families of children with delays and illnesses to find a way to cope with the grief and stress that they face on a daily basis. It is essential that all families deal with their grief so they can dedicate time and energy toward caring for the child and taking care of the family as a whole.

## TRAITS OF PARENTS RAISING CHILDREN WITH SPECIAL NEEDS

Raising a child with special needs is a challenging job. It can deplete a person's energy, contentment, and confidence. Grieving can make parents feel very isolated, but there are many traits that parents of children with special needs all share.

- *Exhaustion.* Every family caring for a child with special needs experiences exhaustion. It can be a full-time job just to make sure the child receives the medical care, therapy, and educational support that he or she needs. When you add the additional time and strength required to work outside the home, care for other children, and take care of personal needs, there is very little energy left. It is essential that families ask for help, whenever possible. Get help when possible, and prioritize what is *essential* each day.

- *Jealousy.* When a child is not like others, it is easy for parents to become jealous of what they see other children doing. It is tempting to be jealous of a little girl who can speak in complete sentences or of a little boy that only visits the doctor for his annual checkup. It is important that parents do not compare their children to others but instead think about their child's specific strengths and how much their child has progressed over time.

- *Lonely.* It is easy for parents to feel they are going through this journey alone. When parents see children and families that look "normal," it is easy to feel as if everyone else has the life they want. Social media can help people to stay in contact with friends and family around the world, but it can also make many people feel more isolated. People typically display their victories and successes on social media. If families already feel alone because of their children's disabilities, then watching everyone else's successes on social media can make the loneliness more intense. Families must remember they are not alone. They need to find others who can relate to the challenges. It can be a relief to the family just to find others who have shared experiences.

- *Scared.* Many families of children with special needs have many fears. They are worried about their child's prognosis. They are worried about the cost of treatment and how to maintain that treatment. They may even be worried about what will happen to their child once the other family members have died. It is okay to worry. Worrying allows our brain to work through the worst-case scenario. The key is not to focus on the worries. Once the family knows their fears, it is important to make a plan. Having a plan in place, even though it will need to be modified from time to time, can reduce feelings of fear and worry.

- *Defensive.* Most parents of a child with special needs naturally want to protect their child. This means it is easy to become defensive when a parent hears terms such as "retarded" or "riding the short bus." Most people who make these types of comments do not know a child that lives with a disability. They make the comment without thinking about how it makes others feel. It falls on the families of these children to educate others about how to be respectful. When others learn how to ask you respectful questions about your child and your family, it can reduce the need to be defensive.

- *Imperfect.* Although all parents try to do their best, it is impossible to make perfect decisions on each matter regarding children. It is impossible to expect anything different from the parent of a child with special needs. The job of parents or the caregiver is to do the best they possibly can with the time and resources that they have available and to ask for help when they need it. It is okay to make mistakes, and it is foolish to expect perfection.
- *Private.* It can be challenging for parents to talk about everything that is going on in the life of their children. This may be because they don't feel others will understand the entire situation, but it is also hard for parents to relive the story again and again. Instead of talking about the child's disabilities and challenges, parents need to talk about all of their children's positive traits. What do they do well? What do they enjoy? Obviously, it is important to give constant updates to doctors and therapists, but outside of these appointments, families need to find a new way to view their children.

With so many families experiencing the same emotions and challenges, it seems that uniting groups of these families will create the strongest and most educated support group. Uniting as a group can also provide shared resources. When parents look for pediatricians or therapists, they often ask other families who are receiving the same type of services. Some of the information that families can share with one another can include the following:

- Supportive pediatricians and medical professionals
- Occupational therapists, physical therapists, and speech/language pathologists
- ABA (applied behavior analysis) and behavior therapists
- Mental health specialists
- Local play groups and support groups for children with special needs
- Support groups for the families of children with special needs

- Recommendations for schools for children with special needs

## BEING THE EXPERT ON YOUR CHILD

Parents and caregivers must learn to take information from doctors and therapists and use that information to make credible decisions. The family must sit in Individualized Family Service Plan (IFSP) or Individualized Education Program (IEP) meetings and listen to suggested goals from specialists on how to meet the needs of their child. It is easy for parents to feel intimidated and unimportant during meetings regarding their children; however, it is essential for parents to understand that they are the experts on their child. The doctor knows the child's medical history. The teacher or the developmental interventionist (DI) knows the child's assessment results. The parent knows *everything*: the medical history, daily routines like sleeping and eating, likes, dislikes, fears, best days, and worst days.

The doctor and the therapist may see hundreds of children each week, but the family is just focused on their child. They know all the details, so it is essential that the parents speak up when sitting in meetings with professionals. The therapists, teachers, and DIs will offer suggested treatments and education plans based on their experiences with other children, but they *need* the parents' expert advice to see if their theories will work with this child. Families need to make every effort to attend all progress meetings and annual reviews to offer their expert advice and make sure that the child receives the best education, medical care, and support services.

# STORY 5: TOMMY

## Told by His Mother, Amy

I was not a young mother when I finally got pregnant with my son, Tommy. I spent a large portion of my late twenties and early thirties attempting to have a baby and going through rigorous infertility treatment. Then, five years after we stopped trying to get pregnant, I found out I was expecting a baby. Tommy was born when I was thirty-five years old. Tommy was born four weeks early and arrived by an emergency C-section. Although he was early, he still weighed seven pounds and four ounces. (He would have been huge if I had carried him to term.)

Because of my emergency delivery, my husband and I did not get to tell anyone that we were headed to the hospital. The C-section seemed to go smoothly, and when I was leaving the operating room for recovery, I told my husband that I didn't want anyone to meet Tommy or hold him until I had the opportunity to hold him first. While I was asleep in recovery, Tommy had an episode of sleep apnea and briefly went without oxygen. He was taken to the neonatal intensive care unit (NICU). When I finally woke up, I wasn't able to hold him.

The doctors in the NICU noticed that Tommy seemed to be having some type of reflux issue. It seemed as though he was regurgitating all of the formula that the staff were giving him. They placed him on an inclined pillow, and he had to be tube-fed. Tommy spent a total of ten days in the NICU before he was sent home. We also noticed that he was having strange screaming fits where he turned to his left side, became very still, and then would relax slightly before he would scream inconsolably.

Once Tommy was discharged from the hospital, he had his first well-child checkup with the pediatrician when he was twelve days old. While I was holding Tommy in the doctor's office, he had another screaming fit in my arms. The pediatrician asked me about how long Tommy had been doing this, and I explained that it happened twenty-five to thirty times per day. The pediatrician told me that Tommy was having seizures, and we needed to see a neurologist as soon as possible. The hospital had set up an appointment for us with the neurologist before we were discharged, but the appointment was still months away. With the help of the pediatrician we were able to see the neurologist two days later.

Once we saw the neurologist, we began a three-month journey of being in and out of the hospital. We would check in to the hospital for the doctors to treat Tommy's seizures, and after a few days of treatment, it would seem as if things were under control. They would send us home, and the seizures would begin all over again. He was having so many seizures when we were at home that the doctor prescribed medication to administer rectally in an attempt to stop the seizures from lasting too long. By the time that Tommy was close to three months of age, the hospital staff kept telling me to wait just a few more days, because a specialist was traveling in from outside the United States to visit the hospital and that they were sure the specialist would be able to help.

When we met the specialist and he reviewed Tommy's charts, he told me it was obvious that Tommy was only having seizures on his left side. At this point every other doctor had told me that Tommy was only having seizures on the right side. I was so tired and stressed over my son that my patience completely left me.

I began yelling at the doctor that he was not allowed to see my son if he didn't even know what side of his body Tommy was having seizures. I told him he was not allowed to touch my son and that I was taking Tommy home immediately. Then we began to argue back and forth with one another. The doctor told me that if I left the hospital with Tommy without pursuing the proper treatment for him, he would charge me with kidnapping my child. The doctor left, and the nurse, who had much better bedside manner, tried to calm me down. I told her that I was leaving in ten minutes if there was no better information that they could offer me about my son.

After this experience, we left and took Tommy to Cincinnati Children's Hospital. They admitted Tommy immediately after seeing him. The first hospital could only tell us that Tommy was having seizures, but Cincinnati Children's Hospital was able to offer a full diagnosis. They told us that Tommy had mitochondrial myopathy complex 3.

When we arrived at Cincinnati, Tommy was so heavily medicated on all of the antiseizure medication that he wasn't even waking up to eat. I had to wake him up to feed him, and then he immediately fell asleep again. One of the first things the new doctors wanted to do was to reduce his medications. The medications were not reducing the seizures, and he wasn't able to do anything else while taking them since he slept around the clock. Since it is not safe to stop taking seizure medication abruptly, it took us a year to wean him off all of the unnecessary medicine.

When Tommy was four months old, the pediatrician recommended that we begin early intervention. The first member of the therapy team that we worked with was an occupational therapist (OT). Our OT was fantastic! Tommy worked with the same occupational therapist from four months until he aged out of the early intervention program at three years old.

One of the OT's first challenges was to help us feed Tommy. Due to the seizures and previously being tube-fed, it was very tricky to help him learn to eat. Initially, I didn't feed Tommy without the OT's assistance.

Although we had a wonderful experience with our OT, it was more complicated to find a physical therapist (PT) that was a good fit for our family. We went through a couple of PTs before we found someone who worked well with Tommy and with me and my husband. Tommy did not become mobile until after he was two years old. We went to a local orthopedic hospital that specialized in working with young children.

The doctor there told me that Tommy would never walk. No one had ever told me that before. I couldn't even digest that information. Why had no one prepared me for this? I called our OT and asked her why she never told me that Tommy would not be able to walk. The OT adamantly told me that Tommy would walk, but it would take time and a lot of determination. I went back to the hospital to the orthopedic doctor and told the doctor that my son was going to walk.

Initially the doctor and I disagreed about what would be best for Tommy. The doctor wanted to put Tommy in a wheelchair. I did not want this to happen. I felt that if he was in a wheelchair, he would never try to walk. The doctor said that while Tommy was nonmobile, he was missing out on exploring his environment. Since young children learn by exploring the environment, he was missing out on the opportunity for additional brain development by being stationary. I understood the doctor's point, but I just did not feel it was the best solution for Tommy.

The occupational therapist had talked to me about why leg braces would benefit Tommy and help get him to a point where he could eventually be mobile. I was set on this plan. The doctor and I had several heated conversations, but eventually she did agree to put Tommy in leg braces.

When Tommy was three years old he took his first steps with assistance. Once he was able to take steps with supports like holding an adult's hands, the next step was to move him to a walker. I was determined that Tommy would be able to use the walker, but the discussion about the walker started another round of debates.

The orthopedic doctor was worried about the risks of Tommy getting hurt using the walker. I was also fighting with the insurance company because they did not want to pay for a walker. It took several months of fighting before Tommy had his first walker. Once he began using the walker, it was only one month until he could walk on his own. Tommy has always had issues with his confidence. The walker helped him see that he was capable of walking on his own. Once he knew he could do it, he never looked back.

Because I am a mother who works full time outside of the home, Tommy has been in childcare since he was very young. Tommy had a very negative experience at his first childcare center, but I was determined to get him into a high-quality childcare program. I found a respected childcare program close to our home, and I continuously called them to see if they had a spot open for Tommy. I would call and tell them about what was going on with his health and his current childcare center, and eventually they moved him to the top of the wait list so he could get into the center as quickly as possible. We were so thrilled when he was finally offered a spot.

Although the center was fabulous, there are always a few bumps in any journey. We did struggle with one particular classroom that he was in during his time there. Because of his delays, it took Tommy much longer than most of his peers to toilet train. Once he was old enough to be in a young preschool classroom, his friends were able to use the toilet independently, but Tommy still needed a lot of assistance.

The teacher in that classroom wanted Tommy to be held back in a younger classroom since he was not able to use the toilet. I wanted him to continue to be challenged. I felt that if Tommy was around children his own age doing more challenging things, then he would be more likely to challenge himself. I went to the program director and explained all the reasons Tommy should get to stay in the older classroom with all of his peers, and the director supported my request.

Tommy's occupational therapist was not only a great asset to Tommy but also a huge resource for our family. Once a child in our state ages out of the early intervention system, then the family must consider two options for continued therapy: applying for public school preschool to receive therapy or paying for therapy at our own expense with insurance or out of pocket. We have private health insurance for Tommy, and we have always had health insurance for him. The only problem is that most private insurance companies only allow a client to have so many therapy visits a year.

If you have a high-quality insurance plan, the insurance may allow you to have twenty visits to an occupational therapist per year. This may be more than enough therapy for someone who is recovering from an illness or an injury. A child with a chronic condition or a diagnosed disability needs to see multiple therapists more frequently than that. Our occupational therapist helped me navigate the Medicaid application process and fight for Tommy to get a disability waiver. Even though we only use Medicaid for Tommy's therapy, it has been a huge asset.

By the time that Tommy was three years old, I had already had to fight for him so many times. I fought with doctors for the best treatment. I fought with the specialists to explain that my child could do more than they expected from him. I fought to get him a physical therapist that could help him excel to the best of his ability. I fought to get him into the childcare program that I wanted. I fought with our health insurance company to provide him supports like his walker, and now I was fighting for him to get Medicaid.

I had not anticipated waiting until my midthirties to be a mother, but I don't know if I could have been the advocate that Tommy needed when I was younger. I would have been worried about making someone upset with me and not stood up for my son. In my thirties, and now in my forties, I have no problem fighting for my son and what he needs. It has become my first instinct.

I waited until Tommy was four years old before starting him in public school preschool. One of the main reasons for this was that public preschool in our town is only three hours per day. If you are a parent that works outside of the home, it can be very challenging to arrange transportation for your child. Once we decided to participate in preschool, we found out that Tommy would not be placed in our local school district. He would be in a school close to our district, but not the one we had hoped he would attend. Since the school was a little bit farther from our home, it was also a little bit farther from Tommy's childcare program. Tommy would need to spend the remainder of my workday at childcare, so the preschool bus would need to take him to the childcare program when preschool was over.

I spent a lot of time on the phone with the public school bus garage trying to arrange this. The childcare program was in the cul-de-sac of a short street in the back of a local neighborhood. The bus garage wanted to drop Tommy off at the beginning of the street, which meant he would have to walk down the street to the back of the cul-de-sac. That wasn't an option for him. After many more arguments, the transportation department agreed that the bus could pull up in front of the childcare program and the teacher could come out to help Tommy get off of the bus.

Public school preschool allowed Tommy to work with a trained early childhood special education teacher and therapists for free, but we still struggled with the experience at times. One day I received a phone call from Tommy's childcare center after he had gotten off the bus from preschool. When he arrived at the childcare center that day, he had a black eye and a huge scratch down the side of his face. I immediately left work to go see him.

Tommy has always struggled with his language skills, and he did not have the communication skills at that point to tell me what had happened to him. I decided to call the school to ask them how my child had gotten hurt. The teachers told me that Tommy had shown up that day with a black eye, but I would have noticed if my child was obviously hurt when I dropped him off at school. I then called the bus garage to see what happened.

The bus driver and the assistant that took Tommy to childcare every day kept a detailed log on the bus in case they were ever questioned about this type of situation. They had written down that Tommy was injured when he got on the bus to go to preschool.

At this point, I decided to call the school again and speak with the principal. The principal reminded me that public school preschool is filled with children who either have a developmental delay or who are at risk of having a delay. For some children, these delays may result in aggressive or uncooperative behavior, not to mention that preschool-aged children are still learning how to share and play in groups. I told her I understood that, but I was just concerned that my mostly nonverbal child had been injured and no one could explain what had happened to him. I never found out why he had been hurt.

When Tommy was old enough to go to kindergarten, he was transitioned back to our district elementary school. The beginning of the school year was not overly hectic because Tommy already had an Individualized Education Program (IEP) from public school preschool, so we did not have to start the year with evaluations and writing an IEP. Even though we didn't have to create an IEP, we still had to have regular meetings.

I hated attending Admissions and Release Committee (ARC) meetings. It seemed the committee spent the entire time telling me negative things about my child, focusing on what he couldn't do instead of how they were going to help him. At one point, the kindergarten teacher contacted me about an upcoming meeting, and I told her I wasn't going to come. I told her I just couldn't sit through another negative meeting talking about what my child can't do. She promised me that this meeting would not be like that. I told her I would attend, but if it became a negative list of my child's attributes, then I would get up and walk out. The meeting went as she told me it would. Every year it has gotten a little bit better.

Tommy continues to grow and change. He has walked as far as four miles at one time. That was actually a hike, so it was a strenuous walk, not on flat, paved ground. He still has a difficult time speaking, but he continues to work on it. At five years old, Tommy joined the Miracle League, a local baseball league for children with special needs. He is not great at baseball, but he thinks he is great. It is helping him so much.

The Miracle League field is right in the middle of a large baseball league where most of Tommy's friends at school play baseball. When they see him playing, it makes him seem more like them. They stop and watch to cheer him on after their own games are finished. It has been a wonderful experience for him. The Miracle League is a resource to families who have children with special needs. When we come to the games, we all cheer for each other's children because we understand their accomplishments. It can be a safe place to be around people who understand what you are going through.

Even though the Miracle League feels comfortable for our family, I continue to push Tommy to try things that are uncomfortable. I want him to be around children who are typically developing and to feel what the real world is like. Tommy has started to participate in his elementary school's running club. He is slow and steady when the other children start off the race at a sprint. He will come home and tell me that he is the worst runner. I always respond by asking him if he did his best and telling him that is all that he can expect. Tommy is usually drawn toward adults, so it is often pushing his comfort zone to spend more time talking to children his own age instead of his teachers.

Tommy has had some amazing teachers, but he has also had teachers who have not been completely invested in the field of special education. When Tommy had only been in elementary school a few years, I received a phone call from the school one day during a meeting. One of the school staff members left a message on my phone saying that Tommy had pooped in his pants and that he was in the office waiting for me to come and assist him. Tommy was mostly toilet trained at that point in time, but due to some of the issues he has with low muscle tone, he has always had problems controlling his bowels. He just didn't have the muscle control to have regular bowel movements.

I immediately left work, and when I arrived at his school I found him in the nurse's office crying and covered in feces. I had planned on cleaning Tommy up and just taking him home that day because I was too upset to speak to one of the teachers. Before I left the building, the teacher approached me and said we really needed to work on Tommy becoming completely toilet trained. I told her that I admit we have to work on toilet training still but that it was completely unacceptable for me to come to school and find my child sitting in feces and crying. If it ever happened again, I would call Child Protective Services to make a complaint for maltreatment.

Of course, the next year, Tommy had a different teacher. She was amazing, and Tommy grew by leaps and bounds. I admit that I am tough on his teachers. I have high expectations for Tommy. I believe he can do so much when he is challenged. If he has a teacher who doesn't expect anything from him, I will let them know that my son can do more. Once his teachers understand that we have high expectations for Tommy, they have helped him achieve more goals.

I know Tommy is going to struggle. I understand he will have a hard time making friends. I know it is painful not to have friends at school, but I also want Tommy to understand that he has to start conversations with others if he wants to make friends. He can do it, if he understands that is the expectation.

When Tommy was very young, his delays were diagnosed and addressed very quickly. The seizures were the first focus, but then we had to focus on his low muscle tone. The low tone was constant. His entire body just seemed to be floppy. The only exception to this was when he was having a seizure, and then it seemed as if every muscle in his body was tense. The occupational therapist immediately started working on large muscle skills. The low muscle tone has contributed to many different issues for Tommy, including his eye surgery and his difficulty toilet training due to irregular bowel control.

Once Tommy was older he was also diagnosed with attention deficit hyperactivity disorder (ADHD). Tommy is constantly moving and always bouncing up and down. During school he can only work for about ten minutes before he needs a brain break. On the occasion that Tommy wears my Fitbit to school, he averages about twenty-four thousand steps per day and about fourteen flights of stairs because he is always moving and always bouncing around.

His primary diagnosis, mitochondrial myopathy, is a hereditary condition. It is a recessive gene that doesn't usually surface every generation, and it is frequently passed down the maternal side of the family. Once Tommy was diagnosed, we had the option of doing the genetic testing to see which side of the family the diagnosis came from, but my husband and I decided it was better not to know. We just didn't want to be able to point blame at one person. I think that has really benefited our marriage in the long run, not to be able to blame the other person for Tommy's illness.

I think it is very common in families who have a child with a disability that one parent becomes the primary caregiver for that child and the other parent handles other needs in the home. That way there is consistent communication with teachers, doctors, and therapists. One person is the expert on the child's appointments and schedule. I have been Tommy's primary caregiver in our home, but my husband trusts me with his care. We communicate about what is going on, and when I have to fight for Tommy, my husband is there to support me.

There are so many emotions I have experienced since Tommy was born. Initially, I just felt tons of guilt. Did I do this to him? My pregnancy was so rough, and I stayed sick the majority of the time. It seemed as if the only foods I could eat without getting sick were potato chips and granola bars. If I had been healthier during my pregnancy, would this still have happened?

I was in the hospital for seven days, but Tommy had to stay longer. It is miserable to be a parent who gets discharged before your child. I was still recovering from a C-section so I could not drive. My husband had to go back to work, so I was stuck at the house during the day just waiting to go to the hospital to see Tommy. Once my husband walked in the door, I pounced on him to take me to the hospital. He was exhausted after a long day of work, but I told him to eat a granola bar so we could go see our son. We had many arguments in the beginning while we tried to figure out how best to care for our son.

When Tommy was finally home, he was really a good baby except for the screaming fits that we later found out were seizures. Should I have known they were seizures? There were lots of things that happened in the first few years that made me feel guilty. I felt guilty over his condition. I felt guilty about not getting him the help he needed quickly enough, and that was exacerbated when doctors did not know how to help him.

Right now our biggest challenge is still Tommy's speech. Tommy's last ARC meeting was in December. The team told me that in January Tommy will begin using an iPad with a text-to-speech function. He can type and the iPad will speak for him. I fought hard against this because I want him to learn to talk independently. He must learn how to speak. Then the team explained to me that he has to learn to type and to spell correctly for the iPad to work efficiently. It will be easier for Tommy to speak, and the iPad will be the last resort.

Tommy's IEP also allows him help from a scribe. I was against this initially. If someone is writing for him, how will he learn to write? If he doesn't do the work, how will he learn? Then I found out that the scribe only helps Tommy with long passages, but he has to tell her how to spell and when to capitalize. When he does assignments with short answers, he must do all of his own work. The school and Tommy's team have found many different ways to support him in his education (which I am thankful for), but I just want to make sure he is always challenged instead of letting another person or a machine do the work for him.

In general, our family and friends have been very supportive of Tommy. There have been family disagreements about what treatment or what doctors are best for him, but everyone was only looking out for Tommy's best interests. In general, even if they don't know what Tommy is doing week to week in school or therapy, they still celebrate successes with him.

There are times when I still get frustrated with people in our community. People will assume that their ten-year-old is older than Tommy since he acts two or three years younger. There were years that I experienced self-pity when my friends and their kids were off doing things together. I just had to realize that their children were interested and involved in different things. We still make an effort to participate in some activities together, even if Tommy's activity is adapted. We can all go to the local trampoline park together. Tommy might not be able to play dodgeball with the other children, but he can still jump on the trampolines with everyone else.

Our church has been very supportive of Tommy participating in lots of activities, but I did have to make an appointment to sit down with our children's leader and explain the types of activities that Tommy was capable of doing. Once they understood what he could do, it was much easier to help him be a part of the curriculum and the group.

There are lots of local businesses in our neighborhood that know Tommy. I send him into the gas station and the neighborhood dough-nut store to order by himself, and he is able to order. He orders at restaurants, but he speaks quietly and people must pause and listen. Most people that are familiar with him can understand him. When people don't understand him, they will frequently look to me to inter-pret what he said. I always tell them that you need to listen to Tommy when he talks even if you can't understand it all. How would you feel if someone ignored you all the time?

There are so many amazing things about Tommy that I wish every-one could see when they are around him. Tommy is a very passionate person. He gives 100 percent of himself to his interests. Right now he is focusing on NBA basketball and knows statistics that no one else knows. He can memorize anything if he is intrigued by the topic.

Math is his favorite thing at school right now. He says that he is a math rock star. I love that Tommy enjoys hiking! Who would have dreamed that a kid who didn't walk until he was three could go on a four-mile hike? He loves the running club at his school. Because he runs steady the whole time, he will pass other children that get worn out from sprinting at the beginning of the race. Tommy is funny. He's just a good kid. I wish everyone that meets him could see that about him.

I think other families need to know that the key to being happy when you are raising a child with a disability is to accept your child for who he is. Even people without disabilities are going to have challenges in life, so it is ridiculous to fixate on your child's delays at a young age. We all go through challenges. When you have your first child, you naturally want your baby to be perfect. The reality is that no one is perfect.

It is also important to find a village of people to trust to help you raise your child. That village may be family, but it doesn't have to be. Just find people you can trust and who accept your child.

I also want to encourage all families to schedule times to meet with your pediatrician when your child is not sick. This time can be so impor-tant to get information from them about the future. Make sure you are comfortable with your pediatrician, and anyone else on your child's team. If you need to fire a doctor or a specialist, do not feel guilty about it. Find someone who believes you and in your child. More than any-thing else, I do not want to be the person that holds Tommy back from achieving everything he possibly can. I am going to challenge him and believe in him. I hope that everyone else in my village can do the same for my son.

# 6

# ALPHABET SOUP

## The Language of IEPs

**W**hen a family begins the process of early intervention or any type of special education support, they are immersed in a flood of new acronyms and new vocabulary. Special education teachers and therapists always try to explain terminology, but sometimes the pace of a special education meeting can leave parents confused and full of questions. It is essential for all families to learn as much of the terminology (and the meanings) before sitting down to important meetings that will set goals and objectives for their children.

## CREATING A PLAN

Once a child has been evaluated and it is obvious that the child needs additional support, the next step is to create a plan to set realistic goals for the upcoming school year and help the child achieve those goals.

### Individualized Education Program (IEP)

IEPs are plans for children three years of age and older. The plan is created to clarify the services that will be offered to the child over the next year and to define the goals and objectives set for the child. The document gives a description of the child's present level of performance

(PLP) in the different areas of development including language skills, academic skills, vision skills, hearing skills, health status, social and emotional skills, and transition skills.

The document will also include information about any assistive technology or specific accommodations the child may need. The document will include information about where the child receives services, specifically if the child receives support in an inclusive environment or if the child receives support in an individual setting. This is a written document required for all children receiving special education services as required by the Individuals with Disabilities Education Act.

## Individualized Family Service Plan (IFSP)

The IFSP is similar to an IEP, but it is created for children under the age of three years old. The IFSP is used to create a plan for a child receiving early intervention, and the plan incorporates the entire family instead of just the child, like an IEP. Just like the IEP, the IFSP describes the child's present level of performance (PLP), describes the type of special education services the child will receive, and describes the goals established for the child to achieve.

The IFSP describes where the child receives early intervention services and how frequently. When a child is under the age of three, early intervention services are typically offered in the child's natural environment instead of in a clinical setting. The IFSP offers services to the child, but it also tries to provide supports to the whole family to make sure the family understands how to take care of the child.

When an IEP or IFSP needs to be created for a young child, it all begins at an ARC meeting. At the ARC meeting, a team of professionals and family members sit down with concerns and make a plan to assess the child and create a plan to help the child develop to his or her full potential.

## Admissions and Release Committee (ARC)

The Admissions and Release Committee is a committee that plans and makes decisions regarding the evaluation, placement, and goals for the child's most appropriate education. The ARC includes the family of the child, the classroom teacher (or developmental interventionist for a child under the age of three years), a special education teacher, an administrator or a representative appointed by the administrator, and therapists that offer the child support in the classroom. If it is appropriate, based on the age and ability of the child, then the child may also be a member of the committee.

When the committee initially meets to analyze a concern, the initial plan may include using response to intervention (RTI).

## Response to Intervention (RTI)

This means the teacher may attempt to change the way he or she is teaching the student in order to help the child learn the concept more successfully. RTI is usually a step that precedes the child receiving formal education supports such as scheduled time with a therapist or special education teacher. RTI is used for students with and without special needs, since all students learn differently. Many students with a diagnosed special need may need more assistance than RTI.

Once the school has identified what type of special education support a student is eligible to receive, then the decision moves on to the parents or legal guardians.

## Informed Parental Consent

No student may receive special education services unless the school system has explained to the family, in writing, why the student needs those services. Once the parents have received notification of why the student needs those services, they need to see the contents of the Individualized Education Program and sign off on it, thereby giving consent. Without the parents' consent, the child cannot receive special education.

## INSIDE THE CLASSROOM ENVIRONMENT

Once a child has an IEP in place, then the teacher or the therapist attempts to find a way to adapt the curriculum so that each child can still participate in the classroom activities and learn about the same content. One way the teacher makes these changes is by using accommodations.

## Accommodations

An accommodation is a small change that allows a student with a special need to participate in all of the classroom activities. The teacher could give a child additional time to complete an activity, teach an activity in a different method (using manipulatives to do an activity instead of paper and pencil), or make changes to the classroom environment to assist with student learning.

One goal for many students with special needs is to include them in the typical classroom setting as often as possible with as few accommodations as possible. When an IEP is first developed, a student may require more accommodations and may spend more time with the special education teacher. Even children that need individualized time with a special education teacher or a therapist still need to be included in an inclusive classroom whenever possible.

## Inclusion

*Inclusion* refers to including children with special needs in the same classroom environment as typically developing students. All students will receive instruction from the general education teacher, and the children with special needs will also receive additional support from the special education teacher or other support therapists.

The education style of keeping children with typical and atypical needs in the same classroom is frequently called mainstreaming.

## Mainstreaming

Mainstreaming allows students with different ability levels to be integrated into the same learning environment. Mainstreaming can offer benefits to all students in the classroom. Students with special needs have positive role models and often learn from their typically developing peers. Students with typical abilities can often strengthen their own learning by assisting a peer and reinforcing their own knowledge.

A child's IEP will frequently mention the least restrictive environment (LRE), and the LRE is different for each and every child.

## Least Restrictive Environment (LRE)

In an LRE, the teachers find the opportunity for the child to spend as much time as possible in the inclusive classroom environment while still making sure the child gets the best possible education. Depending on the child's disability and need for support, the LRE can vary a great deal.

A child with mild delays may spend the majority of the school day in the general education classroom, but he or she may still need to spend one or two individual sessions per week with the speech pathologist to get very specialized training. At the same time, a child with more extensive disabilities may learn better in a special education resource room with fewer students, but that child can still be a part of the general education for activities like physical education, music class, lunch, and recess. The least restrictive environment (LRE) is a spectrum that will continue to change as the needs of each individual child change.

When an ARC is considering the needs of a child, they must often consider the child's natural setting for both assessment and therapy treatment. This is particularly essential when working with very young children who have not yet been in a school setting or who are medically fragile and may be primarily schooled in the home.

## Natural Environment

A natural environment is where the child spends a large portion of time and where the child is comfortable. The most obvious primary settings include their home, another family member's home, a childcare program, a local park, a library, a church, or a classroom. A natural setting can also be created by putting familiar items in the environment, such as toys, books, a favorite stuffed animal, or furniture that the child is accustomed to seeing. People can definitely make a child feel comfortable. Parents, siblings, friends, neighbors, and other family members whom the child sees on regular basis can help establish a natural environment.

Finally, a natural environment can also be established by doing activities with which the child feels comfortable. Familiar activities could be daily routines such as eating, bathing, and dressing. Familiar activities can also include playing in the backyard, with board games, or with dress-up clothing. This also means familiar activities like celebrating holidays, worship, or cultural celebrations. The most important thing to remember is that we can't expect a child to assess well or excel in therapy when he or she is not in a natural setting with familiar people.

## THE RIGHTS OF CHILDREN AND FAMILIES

It is extremely important for parents to remember that they are working together with the school district, the teachers, and the therapists to provide the best possible education for their children. Despite that fact, there are times when a parent may disagree with the school's decision on what is best for the child. One of the parent's primary jobs is to be an advocate for the child, which can involve speaking up against the school's decision. The Individuals with Disabilities Education Act (IDEA) took into account that there would be times when parents and school districts would disagree, so that is why due process was created.

### Due Process

When parents disagree with the recommendations of the school district and the other members of the IEP team, they must, using due process, provide a thirty-day written notice of their dispute. There are two different methods to choose from for due process: mediation or a fair hearing.

Due process is one of the guarantees written into the groundbreaking special education law called IDEA.

### Individuals with Disabilities Education Act (IDEA)

IDEA was originally written in 1975 and promised students with disabilities a free and appropriate public education and the right to an inclusive education. Congress most recently reauthorized this legislation in 2006.

### Free Appropriate Public Education (FAPE)

Special education and supportive services like therapy are provided to all children, at the public expense and not at the expense of the family. All children are entitled to this education regardless of their ability level.

## SUPPORT SERVICES FOR CHILDREN WITH SPECIAL NEEDS

When a child qualifies for an IEP or for an IFSP, it is likely that their education/service plan will include more than just working with the primary teacher or the developmental interventionist (in a home-based setting). Most likely, the child will also need additional support.

### Designated Instruction Services (DIS)

DIS refers to instruction and supplemental support that is not provided by typical classroom instruction or work with a special education teacher. This type of support includes physical therapy, occupational therapy, speech therapy, or even supports as specialized as applied behavior analysis.

### Speech and Language Therapy

A speech and language therapist can help children with communication skills, as well as reading and language skills. Assisting with communication skills includes helping a child decode the language that he hears other people speaking and helping him to articulate his own responses. Once a child is in elementary school, a speech and language pathologist may also help a child with reading and printed language.

Many speech therapists work with children who have problems with stuttering or with difficulties articulating certain sounds. The same speech therapists can also assist students with delays like dyslexia or speech apraxia. Qualified speech pathologists have a master's degree in their field and hold a license to practice.

## Occupational Therapy (OT)

The purpose of occupational therapy is to help someone to successfully do his or her occupation. For a child, the occupation is typically going to school. This means that occupational therapists assist children with a wide variety of skills including fine motor delays, sensory processing issues, and motor planning. Occupational therapists also assist children with a lot of self-help skills, such as feeding, toileting, dressing, and other daily routines. When the occupational therapist assesses the child's motor skills and sensory system, then the therapist can create activities that can be practiced in the home or at school. The main goal of occupational therapy is to help children gain independence, stronger social skills, and better quality of life.

## Physical Therapy (PT)

The purpose of physical therapy is to help children achieve their full strength and mobility. This includes developing the areas of strength, balance, endurance, flexibility, and range of motion. Pediatric physical therapists spend a lot of time working with children who have chronic conditions like cerebral palsy or chronic arthritis. Some children will be able to achieve full mobility, but at times the job of the physical therapist is to make accommodations for children that will always have limited mobility.

## ALTERNATIVES TO AN IEP

Not every child with a special need will qualify for an IEP. Some children will have milder special needs or a health condition that does not justify an Individualized Education Program, but the child still needs special accommodations in the classroom. These children may qualify for a 504 Plan, even if they do not meet the requirements for an IEP.

## 504 Plan

This is a formal plan (similar to an IEP) that provides children with disabilities or chronic health conditions the extra support they need to be successful in an education setting. These plans are called a 504 Plan because they are covered under Section 504 of the Vocational Rehabilitation Act, which is a civil rights law.

A 504 Plan is another way to protect children with special needs from discrimination and to make sure they get the support they need to be successful in school. They are different than an IEP because an IEP has the opportunity to provide individualized instruction to meet the needs of the students. A 504 Plan ensures that a student will receive accommodations in order to complete the required curriculum that is being offered. The most common conditions for which students receive a 504 Plan are learning disabilities, asthma, diabetes, epilepsy, and attention deficit hyperactivity disorder (ADHD).

## Vocational Rehabilitation Act

This act prohibits discrimination based on disability by federal agencies, by agencies that receive federal grants and funding, and in the hiring practices of federal contractors. Section 504 of the Rehabilitation Act of 1973 applies to public elementary and secondary schools and prohibits any type of discrimination based on disability.

# STORY 6: BRIAN

## Told by Brian's Mother, Stephanie

**B**rian was born a completely healthy baby. During his first two years of development, he seemed to be a typically developing and happy child. When Brian was two years and three months old, he began walking on his tiptoes. This didn't seem too unusual to my husband and me because our oldest child, Erin, had done the same thing. Erin started walking on her toes around two years, but she outgrew the habit by the time she was three or four. When Brian first started walking on his toes, we thought the same thing was happening again. He was developing a bad habit, but we thought he would outgrow it in time.

As Brian got closer to the age of three, we realized that his situation was more complicated than we initially thought. When I spent time with him I realized that even with my help, he could no longer make his foot bend back to a flat position, even for a moment. In the same way that someone can make a cup shape with his open hand, it seemed as if Brian's foot was actually cupped due to how far his toes were pointing.

When I took him for his three-year-old check-up, I told that doctor that I did not think this was normal, and I adamantly tried to get the pediatrician to understand that something was wrong. The doctor told me this was still within the range of normal and I didn't need to worry yet. I left the visit with a very unsettled feeling. I didn't feel as if the doctor listened to my concerns, and I knew there was a problem.

Two days later I went back to the same pediatrics office, but I had an appointment with one of the other doctors in the practice. This time the pediatrician agreed with me that Brian's condition was not normal. The doctor referred us to a local pediatric therapy office to begin weekly physical therapy. We diligently began going to physical therapy, but no matter how hard Brian worked and how many exercises he practiced, we did not see any progress.

By the time Brian turned four, the pediatrician recommended that he begin wearing braces (during the day and the night) in order to help stretch the muscles in his foot and make it possible for him to flex his foot. Brian had already qualified for public school preschool due to a motor skill developmental delay, so he was attending preschool three hours a day and getting to work with the school physical therapist also.

When he first began wearing the braces, his preschool teacher would call me from school to tell me that the copper bolts were busting off of the braces because Brian was so strong and would not conform to fit in the braces. These braces had very strong hardware on them that my son was tearing to shreds. My husband and I were trying to fix the braces ourselves because the orthotics company we were working with only came to town once or twice a month. If we had a problem in between visits, we had to watch a YouTube video and attempt to fix the problem on our own.

Brian could have begun public school preschool at the age of three, but there were no other developmental areas that were causing us concern. It didn't seem as if Brian needed special needs preschool, compared with children who might have delays in multiple areas. When you looked at his evaluation on paper, everything looked great, except that he could not walk correctly. When we had our first Admissions and Release Committee (ARC) meeting, the evaluation results didn't seem to warrant Brian receiving public school preschool as a child with a developmental delay. Then I brought Brian in to meet the team, and immediately they understood why he would qualify for services.

After working with the school physical therapist for a while, especially dealing with fixing the leg braces every time Brian broke them, she told me that Brian needed more help than she was able to offer. I was referred to a local pediatric orthopedic hospital that specialized in tough cases like Brian's. I hoped that the specialists at this hospital would have all the magical answers for which I had been waiting. Unfortunately, the whole experience started off differently from what I had expected.

Brian had a scheduled appointment for that day, but due to an extremely large caseload, we ended up waiting in the lobby for six hours before the doctor even saw us. By the time we got to see the doctor, Brian was ready to leave the hospital immediately. When the doctor spoke with us and reviewed Brian's case, she told us that she saw two distinct possibilities: having surgery to cut his Achilles tendon or doing Botox injections to alter the muscles. The doctor also suggested that unexplained toe walking occurs frequently with extreme cases of sensory processing disorder and autism and suggested that may be the root of the problem.

At this point, Brian had been given the unofficial diagnosis of idiopathic toe walking. The diagnosis was unofficial because in order for any condition to be labeled "idiopathic," every other possibility has to be ruled out first. We did not know why Brian was walking on his toes, but I had read enough about sensory processing disorder and autism to know that Brian did not show any of the other signs, except for the toe walking. I did not want my son to have a complicated surgery that may or may not be the solution to his problem, so I decided to look for help somewhere else.

As I sat down at the computer to begin research on who could best help my child, I was willing to drive anywhere and go see anyone who could truly find a treatment. I looked at information from many large hospitals across the United States. As I learned more about idiopathic toe walking, I realized that the predominant expert on the topic was a doctor located in Australia. I emailed this specialist to ask questions, and the Australian doctor told me that there were two doctors in Tennessee at Vanderbilt's hospital that had been doing research on idiopathic toe walking. That was only four hours away from us. When I reached out to Vanderbilt, I was told that one of the two specialists had transferred to Cincinnati Children's Hospital, only two hours away from our home. I had considered taking Brian to Cincinnati before, but this information motivated me to take him there immediately.

Brian finally began treatment at Cincinnati Children's Hospital right before kindergarten. By this point my husband and I felt it was urgent to get treatment immediately. When I had done my internet research on the condition and treating physicians, I read a lot of information on how leaving toe walking untreated can cause degeneration to the hips, spine, and surrounding muscles.

The summer before Brian started kindergarten, we took a family vacation to the beach. As we watched our three children play on the beach, we realized that Brian could not walk on the sand without falling. Of course, sand is not a stable surface, but we could tell that Brian's ability to balance was growing weaker. Before we left the beach to come home, I was approached by a woman who told me that her son had the same condition as Brian when he was a young boy. She urged me to get him help because it was a difficult process to resolve, especially the older the child got before treatment. We were determined that we needed to go to Cincinnati and get further help.

When we first went to Cincinnati Children's Hospital we met with the pediatric orthopedic specialist. Her initial evaluation was that Brian needed serial casting, and possibly Botox injections. Before we could get our insurance to cover the serial casting for an idiopathic condition, we had to get the neurology department and almost every other department to sign off that nothing else was wrong to cause this problem. After meeting with several of the departments in the hospital, we met with the rehabilitation specialist. While we were in her office, the specialist told us that her daughter had many of the same problems that Brian was having, and with her plan of treatment, her daughter was doing fine now.

We began the serial casting process one week after Brian turned five. The idea of the casts was to flex Brian's foot as far as it could go and keep it in that flexed position for a week of time. Brian's muscles were going to be exhausted. The doctor said to imagine stretching your joint out past the point of comfort and being stuck in that position. As she explained this process, she also began to prepare us for worst-case scenarios. She told us that she had only seen one case as severe as Brian's that had been successful with casting. Overall, she was preparing us for the possibility of some very dramatic surgeries that would require the doctors to cut the muscles for a muscle-lengthening surgery. The surgery on Brian's Achilles tendon was also a possibility if nothing else worked.

The first cast had a large wedge underneath Brian's foot, and as the casting process progressed, the wedge became smaller and smaller. We drove back to Cincinnati each week to recast. Serial casting usually lasts six weeks at a time. It is too tiring for the muscles to work that hard without a break. The hospital suggested that we try eight weeks to continue the progress for a little while longer, and we were willing to see if it would help.

When we began the seventh week of casting, Brian screamed all the way home from the hospital. We had to stop halfway home to get ibuprofen, but it did not help. When we got home I called the doctor and explained what had happened for the past two and a half hours. She told us to throw the casts away and take a week break. The next week we were back in Cincinnati, and Brian was getting fitted for new casts.

After we were done with the first round of casting, we had to go immediately to see the orthotics specialist so that Brian could be fitted for leg braces. Without the braces to keep his feet in place, he could easily regress from the process made by the casting. The orthotics specialist has been amazing. Even though we are not in the same town, he checks in with us regularly, and as Brian grows, he makes sure Brian has new braces that fit him at all times. The orthotics specialist also communicates frequently with the doctor who creates the casts to make sure the braces are specifically designed for Brian's needs.

After the casting, Brian was able to put his feet flat on the ground for the first time in years. Only a few months ago, during first grade, we were able to buy Brian a pair of normal tennis shoes from the store instead of ordering him a specialty pair online. It is amazing to see how this wonderful team of specialists has worked together to benefit our son.

The main thing that has made us successful through this process is Brian's determination to work hard. Anyone who knows Brian knows that he is obsessed with baseball. His obsession seems a little overwhelming at times, but I am actually very thankful for it. Brian has been determined to play T-ball and play coach-pitch little league. That is the biggest reason he has worked so hard at physical therapy, done his exercises, endured the casts, and dealt with the braces. He wants to be a better baseball player. He wants to run faster. He wants to be better at the sport that he loves, and that has been his driving force through this entire experience.

As Brian began kindergarten, we had the annual meeting for his Individualized Education Program (IEP), and it was obvious, by academic standards, that his condition was not impacting his education, so he no longer receives special education services from the school system. The principal did ask us if we wanted to pursue a 504 Plan, but at that time, it didn't seem necessary. Instead, I met with all of the teachers, including his specialty teachers, and I let them know that as long as they communicated with me about what was going on, I was not going to pursue a 504 Plan.

One of our biggest concerns was that we never wanted Brian to be in the middle of a crowded hallway at a high traffic time like dismissal or a fire drill. If he is wearing large casts or braces and falls, then he or another student could easily get injured. I explained to all of his teachers what to do if his braces break, and I asked them to text me or call me with immediate needs. Up to this point, the school has done a great job communicating with our family and honored all of our wishes.

Although the casting process was extremely successful for Brian, it did have many emotional side effects that I was not prepared for Brian to experience. The pain and the stress of those weeks seemed to have made Brian very anxious and temperamental. He even seemed mean at times. We have now begun taking him to counseling to work through all of these emotions and tantrums that he experiences. Before the process he was a very happy-go-lucky child, but you can tell that the medical trauma has really been hard on him emotionally.

After the casting was complete, we watched Brian get more and more anxious over the course of the spring. He was asking his kindergarten teacher about what score he received on the achievement tests, and if his score wasn't perfect, he got very upset with himself. If he made any type of mistake playing baseball, such as getting out before making it to the next base, then he would beat himself up over it. Before this experience he was a brave and outgoing child, but I noticed that he was now slow to warm up to new situations. The therapist thought it had to do with his medical trauma and him associating the pain of the casting process with things just not going right.

This anxiety seemed to hit its peak in the summer. Brian's baseball team was at a Saturday competition, and a ball went past him into the outfield. It was a hard ball for any six-year-old child to catch, but Brian became so overwhelmed that he walked off the field. He went into the dugout and threw a hysterical fit. At that point, we knew he needed a break from stress in general. We decided that he was not finishing the tournament that day and we were going home.

We knew that other families disagreed with our decision that day, but we also knew that this behavior was not Brian. He had placed himself under so much stress that he wasn't acting rationally anymore. We finished the last couple of weeks of the baseball season, but then we put everything away for about six weeks. This was completely unusual for our house. Up until then, there was not a day that Brian wasn't begging his father to play baseball in the backyard or that he wasn't tossing the ball himself. He was so anxious that something he loved was starting to make him miserable, so we just took a time-out for a while.

Through this entire process, whenever there was something wrong, I was just determined that we had to fix it. Persistence is the key to making any progress. When one pediatrician would not support me, I went to another doctor for help. You could probably say I was bullish. Brian is my child, and I was going to do whatever I had to do to help him.

I never took that attitude of "woe is me." I wanted Brian to understand that everyone has struggles and you have to work to improve your situation. I have seen families that have access to resources that will help their children but don't take advantage of those opportunities. I just don't understand why. This is your child. Do whatever you can to help him.

You must fight. I have fought with the health insurance company more times that I can even count, but I have to persist in order to even have the smallest victory with them. If something isn't working, then change it. I was determined not to be satisfied until I saw results.

That doesn't mean I haven't cried. I have cried many times through this process, because I don't want him to hurt. One of the most emotional moments that I witnessed was the day we arrived at Cincinnati Children's Hospital to begin casting. We went to the casting room, and my husband became overwhelmed and started to cry. I just tried to keep on my game face and think "let's do this." During the casting process, I would put Brian to sleep at night and then I would go to my bed and lay in bed crying. I was heartbroken that my son was in pain, but I knew we were doing everything we could for him. The results in the long run were going to be worth it.

If Brian was not the child that he is, the whole process would have been so much harder. His sheer determination is an unstoppable force. That doesn't mean he doesn't get upset. He will ask me what is wrong with him and why he was made as he is. I just tell him we won't know exactly until we meet God one day and ask him. Until then it is important to try our hardest and do everything we can to work hard.

Our friends and family have been wonderful through everything. Several of our family members contacted the Cincinnati Reds baseball team and nominated Brian to participate in the Reds Home Caravan. The professional baseball team showed up at our front door to visit Brian, and he was thrilled beyond belief.

Many people in our family sent him cards and gifts during the casting process. The children at his school and on his baseball team have been very kind. Brian has been extremely hard on himself about his flaws, but his friends have never mentioned it to him.

When he first got his braces after the casting, he was determined he would not wear shorts so that no one could see them. Then he realized his friends did not care about the braces, and he was so relieved. It is only the general public that has ever been unkind. Someone at the pool that I have never met will come up to me and make a comment, right in front of Brian, about why my child walks funny. Those are the worst moments, but anyone who knows Brian has never been unkind to him about his delay.

When people meet Brian in passing, I wish they could know how sensitive and kind he really is. He can be aggressive and competitive, especially in the past few months, but that is not who he really is. He is very compassionate with others, and he wants to make sure everything is fair. If he gets more cookies than someone else, he is willing to give one of his cookies away to make the situation fair for everyone.

The past several years have also made him very empathetic to other children with special needs. At one point he was uncomfortable being around someone with a visible disability, but his time at the hospital has made him very empathetic. I hope that when children and other adults get to know my child they will get to see all of this.

When I talk with other parents I tell them that whenever you are worried about your child, go with your gut instinct. Don't let someone talk you out of being concerned about your child. Start the early intervention process as early as you can, and don't stop until you see results. Be willing to drive to larger cities to get your child the treatment she needs, and do not quit until you see positive results. If you don't see positive results, change the plan. There can always be another option. Don't give up.

# 7

# THE "NEW" SPECIAL EDUCATION

Once a family has been through the evaluation process and fought hard for support services for the child, it can still be very shocking to realize that the child qualifies for special education. Many adults have very distinct memories about what special education looked like in their school when they were growing up. Frequently, the children in a special education classroom never had the opportunity to interact with the rest of the school, so their classroom may have even seemed mysterious to the rest of the children in the school. The only thing other children did know is that those children were separated from everyone else.

If adults have memories from being in a special education classroom themselves, they may still be carrying around feelings of rejection or isolation. It can be very disheartening to imagine your own child qualifying for that type of environment, even if it is obvious that the child needs additional assistance. What every parent needs to know is that today's special education classroom looks extremely different from those of one or two generations ago, especially for young children.

## THE INCLUSIVE MODEL

Now early childhood and elementary school classrooms are set up with the inclusive model. This means that children with and without special needs are placed in the same classroom environment. In previous generations, the school system used a separated model where typically developing students were placed in one classroom or in one part of the school and the children with developmental delays were placed in a separate setting. This design established the idea that special education should be a separate education. It created many negative stereotypes.

Today's special education programs have established classrooms where children with different ability levels can all play and learn together. Although placing the children in the same classroom is one step toward a more beneficial education, more importantly schools are sending a message about inclusive classrooms that is making a huge impact on the educational setting.

When schools allow children of the same age level to play in the same classroom without separating children with different ability levels, it is establishing a foundation that all children in the classroom are valued and are important. Separated classrooms often implemented an unspoken ranking order for the children receiving an education. Inclusive classrooms allow all children to have the same experiences, to participate in the same learning activities, and to be a part of the same group of friends. When early childhood classrooms establish this type of environment, children grow up learning that everyone in the classroom is invited to participate.

The inclusive classroom also establishes that each child has a right to be included. The Individuals with Disabilities Education Act (IDEA) establishes many different rights for young children and families. The children with delays have a right to a free and appropriate education just like their typically developing peers. By starting with the expectation of an inclusive education, children with developmental delays will have access to the same curriculum as their peers and only receive accommodations as they need them.

Even when children are meeting all of their developmental milestones, it is important to remember that each child learns differently. When an inclusive classroom is set up so that the teacher can utilize small groups and individualize the curriculum to the needs of the children, typically developing students benefit also. There are many children who excel in certain developmental skills (e.g., language, motor skills, social/emotional skills, or cognitive skills) but still need additional support in one or two areas. An inclusive learning environment will individualize learning for all students and help typically developing students advance in their weakest developmental areas as well.

When teachers and parents evaluate the benefits of an inclusive classroom, there are several outcomes that consistently come to light:

1. Friendships are created. Children with and without developmental delays learn to interact with one another and begin to appreciate each other despite their differences.

2. Children develop a positive image of themselves and those around them. Children with developmental delays feel pride that they are invited to participate in the same activities as other students, and they learn to respect students who can already master skills they are working on learning. Children who are typically developing celebrate the victories of other students as well as their own.

3. All children are able to learn at their own pace. The inclusive classroom becomes more individualized than a classroom that is completely comprised of typically developing children, so children learn that everyone is different and has his or her own strengths and weaknesses. At the same time, children with developmental delays still have the high expectations of learning the same curriculum as other students, even if it is at their own pace. When teachers set high expectations for their students, children will often work to meet those expectations.

4. Children with developmental delays get to lead a more normal lifestyle. Instead of being separated from others, young children with developmental delays can go to preschool or elementary school and have a more typical childhood without being as isolated from others.

Although educators desire for children to learn developmentally appropriate skills, it is not appropriate for a preschooler to stay in the toddler classroom for several years because she is still working on the same skills as a toddler. It can be very difficult to grow close to peers and see them move on to more challenging environments each year and be left behind. The child needs to be offered developmentally appropriate activities while being in a classroom with same-age peers.

Parents can promote an inclusive environment outside of a classroom setting also. It is important for all young children to spend time with other children who are typically developing; however, the settings can vary. Parents need to take advantage of opportunities such as public library circle time, birthday parties, preschool and elementary school soccer teams, and any activities that encourage a young child to interact with same-age peers.

Again, simply having children in the same physical location is only the first step to an inclusive environment. The parent needs to set up the opportunity for the children to play together, but the adult may also have to guide the child through the opportunity to play. If two small children are sitting on the floor with a pretend barn and plastic animals, then the parent may need to sit down on the floor with the children and help his or her child move the animals around to interact with the other child. A mother may have to help her son understand the rules of sharing when playing with other children, and a father may need to help his daughter communicate with a friend when she needs to tell her friend important information.

When parents start with the expectation of inclusion, they will expose their children to more social situations and include their children in more activities. Even if a child with a developmental delay cannot participate in every part of a play group or soccer game, the child is still learning more than if the family stayed at home. Some activities may be too challenging, especially structured activities like a sport, but it is best to have the expectation of inclusion and only explore other possibilities as a second option.

Some play groups, classrooms, and childhood activities may tell parents that they do not have the support for a child with special needs. In this case, it is essential that families learn to advocate for their children. If parents believe their child can participate, it is essential to explain their point. If the play group needs the parent to offer additional assistance, the mother or father can offer to shadow the child in order to make sure he or she can participate. Each family needs to make sure the child is given the opportunity to be included before being told the child is not capable of participating, even from a socialization standpoint.

## SEE IT, DO IT, TEACH IT / PEER ROLE MODELS

A teaching hospital will typically utilize the "see it, do it, teach it" model while training its residents. First, new physicians will watch more experienced doctors complete a complicated medical procedure while only observing. Once the doctor has observed the procedure, then he or she is ready to attempt the procedure independently while a more skilled physician oversees the procedure. The final step in this procedure is when a doctor knows a procedure so well that he or she can explain it to a new doctor. This allows the physician to instruct someone newer in the field, but she will also solidify her own learning by explaining the procedure to someone else.

Maria Montessori was an Italian physician who began studying the growth and development of young children, and she adopted the physician's "see it, do it, teach it" model to improve early childhood education. She believed that when students were placed in multi-age preschool classrooms with children of different ability levels, they would learn better. The youngest students would get to observe older students doing more complicated activities and learn through observation. The slightly more experienced students would gain enough confidence to attempt and complete the learning activities independently. Then the oldest students in the classroom could solidify their own learning by teaching younger students how to use the materials successfully in the classroom. This same structure can be used in a multi-age classroom and a multi-ability classroom.

Many schools now utilize peer-to-peer teaching, and there are several methods available to use in the classroom:

- Peer modeling is a common strategy used in the early childhood classroom. In peer modeling, children can learn classroom procedures, social skills, and academic strategies from other children in the classroom. The key to using this technique in the classroom is to have a group of children with diverse ability levels so that there are several children who can easily master the classroom expectations. When a teacher is occupied, he or she can send a more advanced peer to assist a student having difficulty. The teacher can also use positive guidance techniques to compliment the student following the classroom expectations and then other students will model that behavior in order to receive the same praise.

- Cross-age peer support is a technique where an early childhood classroom might partner with older students (such as a fourth-grade classroom), where the older students come to the classroom and read to the students or assist them with classroom activities. These older students can be excellent language models and provide the one-on-one attention the teacher may not be able to offer. Although this type of collaboration may only occur occasionally, it is shocking to see the amount of information a child can remember when an older student (whom the child admires) teaches the younger child a new skill.
- Collaborative learning is when the early childhood classroom is set up in a way for students to participate in activities together. One way this occurs is when the classroom is set up so that several students can play and learn in the same center together. It may also mean the environment is arranged for children to sit in groups during academic learning so the children can ask each other questions when a teacher is occupied with helping another student.

Peer instruction can have benefits for the children who are instructing while also benefitting the children receiving instruction. The benefits for the children with a developmental delay can include friendships, increased social interactions, role models for a variety of developmental skills, access to the general education curriculum, Individualized Education Program (IEP) goal achievement, increased classroom expectations, easier access to future inclusive environments, and increased parent satisfaction with classroom teaching techniques. The benefits for students who are typically developing include appreciation of individual differences, appreciation of diversity, respect for others, increased number of friendships, mastery of academic skills due to additional practice, and improved academic skills.

Some students may be hesitant initially to give instruction to a classmate, or they may not have the confidence to give another student instruction if they doubt their own skills. These are two reasons for teachers to begin the process of peer teaching in the early childhood classroom, so that students do not feel uncomfortable with this process in later grades. If children experience peer modeling and peer teaching in some of their first classroom settings, it will not feel awkward at a later age. In fact, if older students came to the classroom to read to them when they were in preschool and kindergarten, then most students will look forward to that experience when they are old enough to assume the other role. This will allow students to build confidence and realize their own competency.

## TEAM APPROACH

When a child qualifies for early intervention, there is a team of individuals that sits down to create the IEP or Individualized Family Service Plan (IFSP) and set goals for the child. Once early intervention services begin, the team can use several different team models to implement services for the child.

- *Multidisciplinary teams.* In a multidisciplinary team, the specialists on the team work independently of one another and attempt to help the child meet the goals that fall underneath that specialist's field of expertise. Because each team member is not working toward the development of the whole child, it can appear that the child's progress is not connected. The child may only make progress on a goal in one certain setting instead of being able to apply the new skill toward multiple situations. It may also cause the progress reports from different specialists to conflict with one another. When the specialists do not have constant and frequent communication with one another, the family is often put in the position to track down information from each individual specialist to interpret the information as a whole.
- *Interdisciplinary teams.* Interdisciplinary teams are formed by parents and professionals who are all working together to meet the IFSP or IEP goals established for the child. The team members utilize form reports sent to one another to share child progress, and then regular meetings are set to discuss the child cases that the team members share. Each specialist is responsible for the goals associated with his or her field of expertise, and team

members do not invade the expertise area of another specialist on the team.

- *Transdisciplinary teams.* Transdisciplinary teams are formed by the parents of the child and the group of professionals who are supporting the child. The transdisciplinary team has specialists from several different fields of expertise; however, it attempts to cross disciplinary lines in order to assist in the development of the whole child, particularly since many of the children's IFSP or IEP goals fall under more than one domain. It is challenging to completely isolate the skills into one domain and in the jurisdiction of one specialist.

Crossing the disciplinary boundaries often leads to more collaboration by the specialists and increased communication by the team as a whole. The transdisciplinary model focuses on serving the child within the unit of the family and allowing the child's development to be interactive between the different developmental areas. All decisions made by the team regarding assessment, goal setting, implementation, and evaluation are made by consensus. All team members are responsible for the child's service plan, but the family and the primary service provider (the service that the child receives most frequently) carry out the service plan with the support of the rest of the team.

The transdisciplinary model is the preferred model of service, but it may not always be possible depending on the individuals that support the child. For example, if a three-year-old child has an IEP through the public school and attends public school preschool but has private speech therapy in addition to her public school support services, it may be difficult to get her entire team to collaborate regularly. The private speech therapist would be invited to attend all of the IEP meetings, but that may not always be possible. The most important part is that even if the team members cannot continuously work together, they still need to work toward the same goals and share information with one another.

## THERAPY IN THE CLASSROOM

The Individuals with Disabilities Education Act (IDEA) states that children should be included in the least restrictive environment as often as possible. This means that the inclusive classroom is the best option as long as the children can learn and grow in that setting. In early childhood education, the occupational therapists, the speech pathologists, and the physical therapists attempt to offer their therapy sessions in the classroom whenever possible because it is the most realistic setting for where the child will need to use the skills that he or she is working toward mastering. Some parents are concerned that receiving therapy in the classroom will create a stereotype or label for their children; however, the atmosphere in the early childhood classroom is very different than in older classrooms.

When a therapist walks into a toddler or preschool classroom for therapy, the therapists typically sit down on the floor with the child and use the classroom materials to interact with the child and work toward an established goal. The children in the classroom view the therapist as another adult in the room to play with them, and frequently all of the children in the classroom want to play with the therapist. The child receiving therapy is thrilled to receive one-on-one attention from an adult with whom he or she is familiar and feels comfortable.

When the therapist comes into the classroom for therapy, the teacher can observe the activities the therapist is doing with the child and attempt to re-create those interactions with the child again and again to practice mastery of the skill. The therapist also gets to see the environment in which the child spends a great deal of time. This allows the therapist to see what is expected of the child and set future goals to help the child be successful in the classroom setting. The therapist can view the relationship between the teacher and the child and offer the teacher suggestions on how to help the child be more successful in the classroom setting.

## THE NATURAL ENVIRONMENT

When the IEP or IFSP team is administering support services for a child, it is most beneficial for the child to be in the natural environment. This is where the child lives on a regular basis and feels comfortable. For some children, the natural environment will be the home, so the therapist or developmental interventionist will conduct regular home visits to provide therapy. For children who attend childcare, preschool, or elementary school, the natural environment can be the home or the school. The therapist may use the classroom as the primary place to administer therapy, but he or she may occasionally conduct a home visit in order to collaborate with the parents as well.

Although the term "natural environment" frequently refers to a setting, it can mean other things as well. The natural environment also includes familiar people with whom the child feels safe interacting. The materials available and the activities provided during the therapy session also contribute to the natural environment. If the child is familiar with the building but does not recognize any of the materials or activities the therapist is using, then it will be difficult to get the best results from the visit. Typically when a therapist introduces a new activity to a child it will be preceded or followed by a familiar activity in order to offer comfort. When a child feels safe and is interested in the environment and the toys around him, he is much more likely to learn, so the natural environment is a key piece of the special education process.

# STORY 7: AMELIA

## Told by Amelia's Mother, Katherine

**M**y husband, Ben, and I had always discussed the possibility of adoption. Even before we attempted to have a biological child, we felt called to adopt. Before Ben and I were married, I had dreamed about adopting a child, and even though I was young, I was already thinking about adopting a baby from China. After Ben and I had been married for a few years, we began talking about starting our family. It did not start off as easily as I had anticipated.

When we initially tried to have children, we struggled with infertility. At first I had a miscarriage. Then we realized we would need some medical assistance to get pregnant. As we started to hit all of these roadblocks, we thought that maybe we should start with adoption and see if we can have our biological children in a few years. Adoption was not our plan B. It was always part of our plan, but we didn't know when would be the best time to adopt.

During this time, we succeeded in getting pregnant with our first son, Seth. We also learned that the adoption process for China required parents to be at least thirty years old, so we did not qualify yet. With more medical assistance, we became pregnant again with twins. After the twins were born, my husband and I debated whether or not to have more biological children. We wanted a big family. We decided that we would try one more time to get pregnant naturally. Surprisingly, we did get pregnant again, but I had a miscarriage at ten weeks. We thought this was our sign to look into adoption again.

At this point we were old enough to complete the adoption process with China, and Ben's job would cover a lot of the costs of the adoption. Within six months of my miscarriage, we entered the medical special needs adoption process for China. To complete the application process, we received a long list of possible disabilities for an adoptive child. We had to rate each condition by stating yes, no, or maybe. *Yes* meant we would be willing to adopt a child with this disability. *No* meant we do not feel comfortable adopting a child with this disability. *Maybe* meant we would consider adopting a child with this disability.

The first potential match that we received was not a good fit. As soon as I read the case, I knew this was not our child. There was nothing significantly wrong with the child, but knowing our family, it just did not seem right. After we declined the first match, it was only one week until we received the case file for our daughter Amelia.

Of course, when we received initial information about our daughter, we received her medical file as well. Even though we had the medical information, we still worried about its accuracy. By the time we received her information, Amelia was eighteen months old. The file indicated that she had a speech delay due to an untreated cleft palate and cleft lip. As the paperwork progressed and we got closer to bringing Amelia home, we requested that the doctors in China not repair the cleft lip and cleft palate. At that point, we thought two more months wouldn't make a huge difference, and if we could do the surgery here, we could be confident that it would be done correctly. Also, if she had the surgery here, she would have our support instead of going through the recovery alone.

Amelia finally arrived at our home just after she turned two years old. She arrived here in February 2015, and her first surgery was in April to repair her cleft lip. After her surgery, our main goal was just for her to feel her lips and get them to make contact. We did reach out to a speech therapist, but she told us we could not begin any type of speech therapy until after her palate was repaired. The surgery to repair her palate was in August when Amelia turned two and a half years old. After six weeks of healing, the doctor signed a release for Amelia to begin speech therapy.

As soon as we began speech therapy, I could tell that more had been working against Amelia than just anatomy, but I truly struggled to get others to understand this. In most speech therapy sessions, the therapist attempts to work with the child one-on-one. Parents either view the therapy session from the back of the room or they sit in a waiting room. Amelia was dealing with the past trauma of abandonment. This was more than just separation anxiety, and she needed her mother to be in the room with her. Otherwise she worried about where I was instead of interacting with the therapist. The speech therapist and I finally reached a working agreement that I would be in the room during therapy sessions.

Even with this accommodation, we spent one year in speech therapy with almost no progress. We had a one-hour appointment once a week, and we spent a full year attempting to get Amelia to master two sounds. Something was not working. Every week I left speech therapy in tears. Amelia would get frustrated when she was not being successful, so she would just shut down during the middle of the therapy session. I knew we were missing something.

Eventually we discovered that Amelia was having some difficulty hearing. In one year, Amelia went through three sets of ear tubes, because she had so much fluid buildup in her ears. During this process we saw three different ENT (ear, nose, and throat) doctors. I wanted them to tell me that we were dealing with more than just ear tubes.

We did find some hearing problems. Once we realized that hearing was an issue, we needed to progress with Amelia's hearing before her speech could be successful. I know the speech pathologist must have thought I was crazy during all of this, but I wanted to make sure my child could hear so she could copy the sounds that she was hearing. Once her hearing started to improve, we were still back in the same situation and Amelia was not progressing. The speech pathologist began to discuss other possible diagnoses with me, including apraxia. I was not willing to accept this type of diagnosis yet.

I went back to the surgeon and we discussed a pharyngeal flap procedure. This would benefit Amelia because with her current anatomy air was slipping out her nose and her mouth did not have a seal. The surgery would develop a functional seal between the nasal cavity and the oral cavity. Typically, this type of procedure would be done a few years later in childhood, but since we were losing time with her speech development, we moved forward with the surgery. The procedure went well, but after this surgery I had the false expectation that I would see an immediate impact. There was improvement, but I had expected the improvement to be more significant.

At this point Amelia was getting speech therapy twice a week: once from a private speech therapist and once from the public school system since she was eligible for an Individualized Education Program (IEP) through public school preschool. The school therapist finally heard me when I said, "She passed her most recent hearing test, but right on the line, the lowest possible score." I was still questioning if Amelia really could hear. The school speech pathologist truly cared about Amelia, so she began to dig deep into possible research. During this process she used a device she called a speaking tube. She placed one end of the tube at Amelia's ear and the other end at her own mouth. Amelia could finally hear what she was saying. Six months after her last surgery, Amelia finally made her first *P* sound.

As we continued with speech therapy, I really began struggling with our health insurance company. I had to fight with them to get all of the speech visits coded correctly so they would pay for Amelia's speech sessions, but with all of that fighting, the insurance company still only allowed us a certain number of visits per year. That may be fine for a child who was having difficulty learning to pronounce certain sounds, but it did not seem right based on Amelia's needs. Several people told me that because Amelia had a cleft lip and a cleft palate, she would qualify for Medicaid. I attempted to go through the process of applying for Medicaid, but it was so discouraging.

Our private therapist just kept telling us to apply for Medicaid because cleft lip and palate would qualify. She did not offer any instructions on how to apply. After speaking with families who had been through the process, I applied to qualify financially first so that our family would be turned down due to income. Then I could appeal the decision based on Amelia's need.

I had been told that I could appeal and receive services through the Michelle P. Waiver, but when I contacted the Medicaid office, no one at Medicaid seemed to know about the Michelle P. Waiver. I have a degree in social work but couldn't navigate the state system for helping families in need. The public school system gave me some guidance on applying for disability through the social security office, but I also had to take care of my family. It took too much time and energy to fight this with little to no outcome. My husband had a flexible spending account through his employer, so we decided to use that for our therapy expenses. That at least allowed us to pay the medical bills tax free.

I was also struggling to work with the private practice therapist. Every visit seemed to end in tears. Our pediatrician was such an asset during this time. He called me at home one night (after hours) and just listened to me cry. During our discussion he recommended that I speak to the mother of one of his patients. She was a speech pathologist. He had given me her card once before, but I had never pursued therapy with her. I learned that she did not take insurance, and I felt we were bound to our current speech pathologist because of the insurance company. I had also reached out to a speech pathologist at a regional children's hospital that was a couple hours away from our home. I sent the specialist at the hospital some videos of Amelia talking, and she offered some consultation without even charging me.

As I became unhappier at our visits with our speech pathologist, I realized that our number of speech therapy visits with our insurance company was about to run out. If we were going to have to pay out of pocket anyway, I might as well see what the other speech pathologist was going to charge. Between the cost of our deductible and the cost we were absorbing when the insurance company bounced back claims for coding issues or other problems, the new speech pathologist would not be much more expensive.

Within two months of treatment with Ms. Rhonda, Amelia's language skills began to explode. Ms. Rhonda found a way to help Amelia be successful. She found a way to help Amelia feel brave during therapy so that she was not stuck to my side during each session. Ms. Rhonda also understood some of the sensory processing issues that Amelia had been having, so we saw fewer tantrums and meltdowns during therapy sessions. Before we started therapy with Ms. Rhonda, Amelia was only speaking with vowels. Ms. Rhonda helped Amelia find and use consonants.

Since Amelia is so petite, people often anticipate that she is much younger than her actual age. At this point, that has actually helped us some. People do not expect her to speak in public or to understand her when she does speak. I was starting to worry about how long that would last. Is she ever going to talk? Can she ever have a job if others can't understand her? Can she live independently if she can't speak?

I felt very alone, going through these emotions each day. I even wondered if my husband completely understood how bad it was at times. He was extremely supportive, but he was at work every day while I was going to therapy visits and doctor's appointments. While I was working hard to help Amelia make progress, I also had three other children in the home whom I was homeschooling.

When we brought Amelia home, we took her file to the adoption specialist. The specialist reviewed the file, and she let us know things that we would definitely experience with a child who had this medical history. She also let us know the possible "maybes" that we could experience. I understood when I adopted a child with special needs that she was going to need surgery and therapy, but I did not anticipate that we would experience everything that had been on the "maybe" list.

Amelia has made some great advances lately, but she will be in speech therapy for a long time, probably well into her elementary school years. Right now I get so excited when other people tell me they can understand Amelia when she speaks to them. At one point Amelia told me that she does not even try to talk to people at our church because no one can understand her. Now people who don't know her that well will tell me she is a chatterbox.

A huge turning point for me in Amelia's therapy process was when we decided to stop using our insurance company and pay out of pocket for her therapy. I love that paying for therapy myself allows me to decide how much therapy my child needs. I get to decide what is best for her. I get to decide how long a session my child needs and not overwhelm her. She can now have forty-five minute sessions, the exact time amount she can handle.

Before, the insurance company allotted me so many sessions, and the sessions could be thirty minutes or sixty minutes. I felt obligated to take the sixty-minute sessions knowing we would eventually run out of approved visits. A sixty-minute session wasn't necessarily best for Amelia. Now the medical professional and I decide on the goals for Amelia's therapy, regardless of what the insurance company wants.

When we entered into the adoption process, we were prepared for the fact that Amelia would have delays, but the level of frustration was heightened because we were trying to bond with a newly adopted child.

The first year was a very dark time for me because I was dealing with so much at one time: adoption trauma, insurance, surgeries, speech therapy, and so forth. I think I prepared myself for the medical part, but I was not prepared to live the emotional part of the adoption. Adoption always starts with trauma because a child is separated from the family. When you add a special need to that trauma, it can be overwhelming.

The whole process feels isolating because you can't just talk to anyone about it. It takes someone who has gone through it to understand the journey. The adoptive community has been like a family, and many times there are things I can share with them that I would never say outside of that group. Others would hear my stories or comments and judge me. They see the pretty picture of adoption, but they don't realize that it starts with a very broken situation and a child that is mad at the world. The same is true with a child that has special needs. You have to have people who have walked the same road you have to really understand how difficult that it is.

More than anything else, it is essential not to give up. Don't take no for an answer. You don't have to damage relationships to be an advocate. If people aren't listening to you, find new people. I was worried about hurting our first therapist's feelings, and I should have left months earlier. I felt we were trapped by the insurance company, and we couldn't get help anywhere else. My husband told me that I didn't need to worry about hurting her feelings. She is a professional, and she will want what is best for her patient. He told me to find what was best for Amelia and not worry about anything else. He really helped me feel empowered, but I wish I had done it sooner. I let it become a big mountain (combined with insurance issues), and it stopped me from doing what I thought was best.

This experience has changed me in so many ways. I have definitely become tougher and more persistent. I started asking questions to anyone I knew who had ever had services for their children. I kept asking people what the next step was when we ran out of options. I know my child best, so I needed to push boundaries. It was a continual sacrifice of time and energy, but it was worth it for my child.

Our extended family has been an amazing support. My parents live far away, and when they come to visit they stay with us in our home. Because I am there all the time during those visits, they always have someone to explain to them what Amelia is saying. Ben's mom lives in the same town and gets to see all of our children on a regular basis. Although she is with Amelia more, she is still apprehensive about keeping her at home alone because she can't completely understand her. Right now she always has Amelia and her big sister come to visit at the same time, and my older daughter can interpret for her if she cannot understand Amelia.

Even though some people in our family still cannot understand her, Amelia is very persistent. She will keep trying and trying. It takes her a long time before she gets frustrated. I get so excited when Amelia talks to people she doesn't know and when she talks to children outside of our family. It is even more exciting when they understand her. She still has a lot of work to do, but we have come so far.

Despite our progress, I do worry about what the elementary school age will bring. I can envision kids telling her that she talks funny or asking her what is wrong with her lip. I am thrilled right now that we are surrounded by loving friends and family who care about Amelia and who support our whole family. I pray that this secure start will help her overcome even more obstacles in the future.

# 8

# THE EARLY INTERVENTION TEAM

In order to write an effective Individualized Education Program (IEP) for a child, a team of experts is assembled. Parents, teachers, therapists, and other professional staff sit down at a meeting to discuss the child's level of development, and then they create an education plan based on the needs of that one child. They use all the information from the child's evaluations, and then they establish realistic goals for the child and determine the level of support services the child will need in order to be successful. Support services can include occupational therapy, physical therapy, speech therapy, or mental health services. The IEP may also indicate if the child needs technology assistance, one-on-one support from an assistant, or other more specific accommodations.

The Individuals with Disabilities Education Act specifically outlines who is required to be placed on the IEP team. The parents or guardians of the child must be included on the IEP team. At least one regular educator of the child must be included on the team, if the child is in an inclusive environment. Also, at least one of the child's special education teachers must be a part of the IEP team.

The team also includes at least one person who can interpret the results of the child's evaluations, for example, a diagnostician. Representatives of a public agency who are qualified to provide special instruction to meet the needs of the child are also invited to attend the meetings. In most cases, this will include speech therapists, occupational therapists, physical therapists, mental health experts, or other experts that can provide specialized services to a young child with a developmental delay or a diagnosed disability.

Other individuals with expertise about the child can also attend the meeting. In many cases, this means that the family may invite a medical professional who treats the child or a child advocate to support the family. The child is also invited to attend the meeting if it is appropriate. This occurs more often when the child is older.

The IEP team has several important responsibilities. Throughout the child's special education experience, the IEP team is responsible for the following:

- Developing the initial IEP
- Meeting annually to assess the child's progress and update the IEP goals
- Administering assessments and evaluations on the child
- Tracking the child's progress toward achieving the IEP goals
- Meeting together when the child has new needs arise
- Advocating for the child to have the best possible education and learning to the best of his or her ability

The Individual Family Service Plan (IFSP) is very similar to the IEP, but it is for children under the age of three years. The IFSP also focuses on involving the family in the child's development, compared with the IEP, which focuses on the child's development in a school-based setting from age three to age twenty-one. The IFSP works to provide early intervention services to the child in the natural environment, so if a child spends the majority of his or her time in the home, then intervention should be provided in the home. At the same time, if the child spends the majority of his or her time in a childcare program, the early intervention team will provide services to the child in the childcare center.

When the team creates the child's initial IFSP, they consider the child's present level of development in order to set appropriate goals, but they also consider the preferences and priorities of the family. They review the priorities of the family and consider what the family is most concerned about for the child. They also consider what resources the family has available already and what needs to be provided for the family. The IFSP tries to utilize the strengths of the family and build on those strengths with the specialists that visit the family.

Similar to the IEP team, the IFSP team includes the following participants:

- The parents or guardian of the child
- Other family members by request
- A child advocate who is not a family member
- The professionals that complete the assessments and evaluation of the child's developmental skills
- Specialists that provide early intervention services to the child and family including medical professionals, mental health specialists, speech therapists, occupational therapists, physical therapists, social workers, or child development specialists.

The IFSP team is responsible for reviewing the IFSP every six months and updating it at least once a year. The team must document the child's progress and the family's progress. As the team observes the child and family, they may need to update the child's goals in order to continue to challenge the child and help him or her to meet developmental milestones consistently.

Each member of the IEP team (and the IFSP team) has specific skills that contribute to the team in order to benefit the child. Based on the knowledge and the skill set of the specialist, they have many different responsibilities.

## THE ROLE OF THE DEVELOPMENTAL INTERVENTIONIST (IFSP TEAM MEMBER)

The developmental interventionist (DI) is an early childhood education teacher who frequently specializes in working one-on-one with a young child. The DI's primary job is to create age-appropriate activities for the child to work on specific skills that are included in the IFSP goals for the child. Instead of only focusing on one specific area of development, as a speech pathologist may do, the DI focuses on helping the child improve in all areas of development, including cognition, language and communication skills, social and emotional development, fine and gross motor skills, and self-help skills. The DI's specific responsibilities on the IFSP team are very similar to those of the classroom teacher on the IEP team.

## THE ROLE OF THE CLASSROOM TEACHER

The classroom teacher spends the most time with the child in comparison to every other professional on the IEP team. Next to the family, the classroom teacher becomes the most familiar with the child and can most easily track the progress of the child's development. That also gives the teacher a great deal of responsibility. As a member of the IEP team, the teacher must

- attend all IEP meetings;
- assess and provide developmental information;
- recommend needed support services and referrals;
- help establish IEP goals;
- provide strategies and accommodations for the student to meet goals successfully in the classroom;
- maintain communication with the family throughout the school year (in between IEP meetings);
- document progress on IEP goals;
- provide updates to the IEP team about the child's progress in the classroom and updated needs; and
- maintain confidentiality and professionalism.

## THE ROLE OF THE THERAPISTS

If the child receives some type of therapy as a support service on the IEP or the IFSP, then the therapist is an important part of the early intervention team. As a member of the team, the therapist must

- attend all IEP meetings;
- provide information about services and eligibility criteria;
- participate in establishing IEP goals;

- develop a consistent schedule for visiting the child in the natural environment (home or classroom);
- create activities (play based) that motivate the child and encourage her to work toward developmental goals;
- teach parents and the classroom staff how to continue working on goals in between therapy visits;
- reassess as progress continues; and
- maintain confidentiality and professionalism.

## THE ROLE OF THE FAMILY

Many families do not feel qualified to be a member of the IEP team, since they are not professionals in the field of education or child development. The reality is that each family is an essential part of the IEP (or IFSP) team because they are experts on the child, and they bring the most important information into consideration. The role of the family on the IEP team is to

- talk about the strengths and weaknesses of the child (they are the experts), including interests, what motivates the child, and how the child learns;
- offer information about the family's priorities and cultural customs;
- share relevant family history and medical information with the team;
- provide permission for further assessment and treatment;
- help create goals as equal members of the team;
- follow through and work at home toward goals;
- communicate with the teacher (home visitor) and the therapy team;
- self-educate on child's delay/diagnosis; and
- advocate and be knowledgeable about the child's and family's rights.

## THE ROLE OF THE SOCIAL WORKER

A social worker is another possible member of the IEP team who can have many different responsibilities. If a child has documented behavioral problems, it is more likely the child will have a social worker instead of a case manager. When the social worker is part of the team, he or she

- compiles a family history during the evaluation process;
- assists the family with behavioral problems identified in the evaluation process;
- documents the child's relationships with family members and other members of the IEP (or IFSP) team;
- may mediate conflicts between the child and other peers when there are disagreements that the child cannot resolve independently;
- assists with implementing district policy in the IEP process;
- provides the classroom teacher with support to interact with the family and interact with the child as the child demonstrates behavioral problems;
- can offer the family additional resources for dealing with behavioral problems outside of the school day;
- can offer the family resources for issues the family may be dealing with as a whole, such as referrals to programs like homeless shelters, food banks, or support groups; and
- maintains confidentiality and professionalism.

## THE ROLE OF THE MEDICAL PROFESSIONAL

Although doctors may not understand the educational system and the requirements of the IEP, they can be an essential part of the IEP team. If a medical professional is on the IEP team, he or she

- provides documentation on the child's diagnosed condition;
- provides information about the possible side effects of certain medications that can be used for treatment of the medical condition;

- provides information about the child's stamina and ability to function in a typical school environment compared to the home environment; and
- supports the family and advocates for the child.

## THE ROLE OF THE ENVIRONMENT

Although the classroom environment is not a member of the IEP team, the *structure* of the environment is an essential component of the child's learning. Followers of the Montessori classroom believe there are three main components for a child to achieve deep learning during the school day: the teacher, the student, and the environment. Each of the three components is equally important to create ultimate learning. When a young child is in preschool or elementary school, the classroom learning environment is where essential interactions occur. The classroom must be set up in an exploratory and encouraging setting. The learning environment is important to the child's development because it is

- the setting where children live, learn, and play—the natural environment for therapy;
- where children (and adults) participate in typical daily routines and activities such as play activities, entertainment, rituals, celebrations, and social activities—more specifically, eating, bathing, playing games, reading, walking, doing laundry, gardening, parties, and visits with family and friends;
- promoting learning in a place that children will use the new skill;
- providing adult and peer role models that will demonstrate new skills;
- providing children with opportunities to practice the new skill;
- recognizing parents and caregivers as the primary influence;
- inclusive for children with and without special needs;
- promoting independence;
- allowing children to participate in indoor and outdoor activities;
- developing all domains (motor, language, cognitive, social/emotional, and self-help);
- open ended and exploratory; and

- providing relationships, choices, time to be alone and not rushed, and challenges.

## COLLABORATING AS A TEAM

When a team of individuals sits down at a table to create a plan for the education of a young child, it is easy for people to have differing opinions. Each professional has a specific goal that they want to help the child achieve, and it is easy for each professional to prioritize his or her goal as the most important. The ultimate reason for each person to be at the IEP meeting is to benefit the child, so it is important for everyone to keep that in mind.

One way to make sure that every team member works cooperatively during the meeting is for each person to come to the meeting prepared. If parents and professionals prepare in advance, then the IEP (or IFSP) can be very streamlined and respectful of each person's time. This means that evaluations must be complete, evaluation summaries written, and goal progress recorded to share with each member of the IEP team. It can be even more helpful for the members of the IEP team to email all of this information to each team member in advance so that everyone has the opportunity to review the information before the meeting begins.

Another very important skill for IEP meetings is for each member of the team to acknowledge the other participants as experts, including the parents and parent advocates. Each person on the committee has very important information to share with the team, so if respect is shown to each team member, the team is much more likely to work well together.

Finally, it is important for all team members to acknowledge that behavioral goals are just as important as academic goals. The education system places a high priority on academic advancement, but if the child is having behavioral challenges, it will be difficult to advance academically. When the committee focuses on the development of the whole child, the child is much more likely to be successful.

# STORY 8: THE CLASSROOM TEACHER'S PERSPECTIVE

## Told by Mrs. Colby, Public Preschool Teacher

**A**s a public school preschool teacher, I have the opportunity each school year to work with a wide variety of children. It is one of the reasons my job is so exciting! I get the opportunity each year to learn about a new group of students. I get to learn about what they like, what they dislike, what is important to them, what they are afraid of, and what motivates them.

During the course of the school year, I notice when I have students who are beginning to excel in our classroom environment, but I also see students who are falling behind the development of their peers. One of my responsibilities as a teacher is to identify students that need special education support. That is a responsibility that I do not take lightly.

In order to get to know my students, I use a developmental screening tool at the beginning of each school year to assess their development level. The screening tool looks at their language skills, motor skills, social and emotional skills, independence skills, and cognitive development. This information is important for every child in the classroom because it helps me to plan activities that challenge each child's individual development.

When I assess a child on the screening tool, and he or she scores lower than the developmental norm, then I know I need to pay closer attention to that child over the next few months. Sometimes a child scores low on an assessment because she is having a bad day, so you can't base everything on one screening. I usually try to observe the child for a couple of months to see if the information on the screening tool is an accurate portrayal of the child's abilities.

If I notice over those couple of months that the child is not making significant progress in the classroom, then I typically seek out a second opinion. Working in the public school system, I have the opportunity to collaborate with a great team of special education teachers and therapists. I usually ask a special educator or a therapist who already spends time in my classroom if she can observe a student whom I'm concerned about. This offers an unbiased perspective. If a member of the special education team sees the same concerns, then it is probably time to invite the parents to a conference or ask if I can do a home visit to talk about the child's progress.

When I do sit down with the family, I always start by sharing some of the child's successes in the classroom. It is essential for parents to hear positive information about their children and to know that I am learning details about their children each day. During the meeting with the family members, I will show them the screening tool we use and the areas in which we assess each child. I will also explain the areas where I have noticed slow progress and try to encourage them to share what they have seen.

I try to give examples of specific situations to set up the conversation in a way to trigger their memories. I might ask questions such as, "Have you noticed that other people can't understand what Andrea is saying?" or, "Does Mark play with other children when you go to the park or when you take him to birthday parties and family gatherings?" Often the family members already have the same concerns that I do, or they could be noticing the same things that I am but they do not know they should be concerned about their observations.

When we have discussed what they have noticed and I have identified my concerns, I ask the family if I can begin to collect data and record observations that may help us support the child. Once parents can think about a specific situation, they may be more willing to open up and share important information that can help in the assessment process. Once we identify the areas of concern, then the family has a better idea of the specific areas about which I will be collecting data. If

I feel the need is significant, then I may speed up the data collection process.

If I have collected data for several weeks and the child is not progressing, it is time to call a meeting and ask the therapists to observe the child. The family is always invited to a referral meeting. The referral and evaluation process can be very lengthy. After the initial meeting, we always ask the family members to fill out a questionnaire to make sure we get their insights regarding their child. The individual team members may ask the parents additional questions to get data for their specific area of study.

There is so much information for the family to absorb during this process. I know that it must be overwhelming. I have watched many families as they try to sort through all the details of the referral process. As a non-family member watching the situation, I have a lot of worries myself. My main worry is that after I sit down with the family members and share all of this information, the family members will disagree with me.

Of course, I have worked with families that feel this way. Their response may be, "No, we think everything is fine right now." This is always the parents' decision, and they have the right to decline services or to wait until later to pursue support. As a teacher, I always hope that the child gets extra support quickly so that he or she will not need it later on.

Most parents are willing to hear my concerns and want to see if their children need early intervention. Sometimes the family members disagree on what is best for the child. That can be upsetting to watch. Ultimately, I want the family to have a unified decision and feel confident about their child's growth and development. Whenever I do present this type of information to the family, I am concerned I might offend them. That is never my intention. My goal is to be considerate and share necessary information with the family. My only reason for having this type of conference is to benefit the child. I always hope that the families I work with understand that.

I also worry about the family feeling blame for the child's delay. I can remember meeting with one mother to explain that her child was showing delays in all developmental areas. My intent was to offer her some hope and tell her about what the school could do to support him. The mother was overwhelmed with emotion and quickly began to cry.

She felt extremely guilty. During her child's short life, the child had already experienced many challenging situations in the home, and it was obvious that this amount of stress had affected her child's growth and development. The mother eventually agreed that we needed to refer her son for special education services, but it was an extremely tough decision for her.

As a teacher I try to support the whole family as they begin the evaluation process, so the family members' reactions to this information definitely affect how I support them. It is easy to be disappointed or upset when a family declines support services for a child, but I never want the family to know I am upset. As a professional, I do not want my disappointment to affect my relationship with the family at all. My goal is still to nurture and teach the child to the best of my ability.

When a family is still very emotional about the process, I try to make sure I am explaining everything that happens, step by step. I also make every effort to celebrate any progress that the child makes. I feel that families get a great deal of encouragement just by seeing slow and steady forward progress. I also continue to explain to the family why it is so helpful to address these delays in preschool instead of waiting for kindergarten. "If we do this now, it will be so much better in kindergarten."

Some families agree to the evaluation process for their children, but they are still very reluctant because of past negative experiences they have had with special education. It could be that an older child had a negative experience, or it could be that one of the parents had a negative experience themself as a child. In these cases I always encourage the family to observe the classroom to see what it is like when one of the therapists comes in to offer therapy. Every child in the classroom wants to play with the therapist. There is no negative connotation to therapy in the preschool classroom. I also want to make sure the parents understand the demands of kindergarten. If I can explain what will be expected of a child in kindergarten, that helps the family members understand what the "goal" for therapy should be.

Occasionally I work with a child who does not need early intervention, but the family believes the child is not developing at the rate he or she should be. I never want to dismiss the instincts of a parent, because they know the child better than anyone. If the family does have concerns, I will go ahead and begin collecting data to see how the child is progressing. If the data show that the child does not qualify for support services, then I try to provide the family with activities they can do at home to help the child.

I do make sure my families know that academic skills (prereading and premath skills) are not the only focus of preschool, so they do not need to worry if a preschool child is not beginning to read or perform kindergarten-level skills. This is another case where I may review the kindergarten expectations with the family to help them understand what is appropriate for the child's age and development level.

If a child in my classroom does qualify for an Individualized Education Program (IEP), then I have a very important role. I spend more time with that child than any other professional staff member. Where a therapist might be focusing predominantly on speech or on motor skills, I am the professional that focuses on every area of development and working with the whole child. I see the child in a group setting with other children, which is different than most therapists and the family.

My relationship with the family is crucial compared to the rest of the Admissions and Release Committee (ARC) team. I want them to trust me. I support the entire family. I let them know that I will go with them to the ARC meeting and it will be okay. I always try to explain things to the family that they don't understand. These meetings can have very tricky terminology, so I want to make sure that every family in my classroom understands the discussions we are having related to their children.

A large part of my job as the classroom teacher is to collaborate with the other members of the special education team to make sure each student gets the best possible education. The child's IEP states his or her goals, so I have a general idea of what each therapist is working on with the child. The problem is that the therapist only gets to see the child once or twice a week in the classroom to work on these goals. That means I have to make sure my classroom is set up for children to meet their goals. I ask for suggestions from the therapists about which strategies I can use to meet the child's goals and how to change those goals if he isn't progressing. I want them to give me hands-on examples of how to do these activities in my classroom so I can implement them correctly.

It is also essential that I continue to communicate with the family. The school requires that progress reports are sent out every nine weeks.

This is a great way to receive formal information, but it is not enough information to keep the family informed. I work really hard to establish a relationship with the family so we can have casual conversations frequently. I talk about what I am doing during the intervention process, and I give them ideas for activities to do at home.

During home visits I ask parents for their goals and hopes for their children that can be put into the IEP goals. We have monthly family story times, so I get to see the families frequently. I use those times to show parents activities that we are doing in the classroom and show them activities at which the children are able to be successful. After the formal reports, I always ask parents if they have questions about the technical terms, and if they do, then we can set a time to meet and go over their questions.

More than anything else, I want each of my families to know that I care about their children. This is not just a job for me; it is a passion. I do it because I want to take care of these children and help them be successful. I also think that early childhood is the most important developmental stage for a child, and so many people don't understand this. I chose this field because I want to help children when their brains are growing the most. Letters are not the most important. I want them to solve problems and have conversations.

This is a hard time to be a parent. It is hard to know how to help your children the most when they have limited vocabulary and still throw tantrums when they do not get their way. I want to support families while they figure this out. Kids are still learning emotions, and I want to show parents how to deal with those emotions. Raising a child is such an immense job, and I want to be there to support the parents and the children. I hope that all the families I work with know I am here to help.

# 9

# THE PARENT'S ROLES AS ADVOCATE

The parents of a child with a developmental delay have the responsibility to ensure that their child is receiving the best possible education, including the appropriate support services to support the child in the classroom.

## WHAT DOES IT MEAN TO BE AN ADVOCATE?

When parents first begin to advocate for their child, it is essential to begin the advocacy journey with three foundational skills. First, it is very important that all parents educate themselves about the children's particular developmental delays. This can mean asking the pediatrician for information or doing independent research. The internet offers a wide variety of information about many different developmental delays, but it may not always be accurate, so parents must double-check if the source is reliable and the information is current. Along with education on the child's condition, the family must learn about special education law to ensure that the child's rights and the family's rights are protected. Most school districts have a parent resource office with a parent advocate that can explain special education laws and rights to families. Also, local community groups such as your regional Down syndrome association will have parent mentors that can assist families in learning the legal responsibilities associated with Individualized Education Program (IEP) meetings.

Parents need to make a dedicated effort to collect documentation about their children. From the time that a parent begins to notice developmental differences, it is critical to start taking notes about the child's development. As the parent begins attending meetings, it is important to save all official paperwork, including assessments, evaluations, recommendations based on the evaluations, and updates provided by the specialists.

Parents need to maintain copies of the IEP to make sure they understand what goals the school is working on with the child and how many services are offered to the child. The family members should make sure to store all of this information in a place that is easily accessible, but the family members also need to remember that they can ask the school to provide an additional set of the IEP and other evaluation reports at any time.

It is best for every family to keep its own set of documentation to hold the school and the IEP team accountable, but if those records are lost, the school can provide the family with another set of records upon request. The parent's documentation also needs to include the child's response to certain therapies and a documentation log of how you are implementing exercises or activities in the home. Then, if the intervention is not successful, the parent can provide the information to the IEP team to show that the plan needs to be adjusted.

Advocates learn to be experts on certain topics. To advocate for a child's education and special education plan, the parent needs to learn about the local school system and find out who makes decisions in the school system. Advocates also know the child's rights and the parent's rights, and an advocate will bring up those rights in meetings when someone on the committee is not following the proper procedure. In fact, a true parent advocate does not even expect the school staff to review the rights and responsibilities of the family. Many parent advocates take it upon themselves to learn their rights on their own, even though the school is required to provide the family with a brief description of these rights.

An advocate is a question asker. This means that not only is the parent unafraid to ask a plethora of questions to doctors, teachers, and other school personnel but also the parent learns *how* to question the specialists in order to learn about the child, the school procedures, and the education that the child is receiving. In order for an advocate to learn to be a question asker, the parent or guardian must think back to his or her own elementary school language classes and think through how to create questions. The parent needs to have lists of questions that include who, what, when, where, how, and why in order to learn about every aspect of a child's education.

When advocates learn to ask questions, they can use the information from those questions to brainstorm with the educational professionals. When parent advocates know their child is struggling, they need to brainstorm possible solutions and discuss those with the IEP or Individualized Family Service Plan (IFSP) team. This is important because parents protect children in a way that no other adult can, so if the parents assist in problem-solving, they bring an additional passion to the problem-solving process. Passion encourages new ideas and drives timelines so that children get the support services they need.

Finally, it is necessary for parents to reach out to establish a close working relationship with their child's teachers. This relationship is crucial in order for the parents to get continuous updates on how the child is progressing toward his or her IEP goals. The family and the teacher must establish the best way to stay in communication, whether through email, phone calls, or written communication, and then they both need to make a commitment to share information with each other on a regular basis.

## WHEN DO I NEED TO START ADVOCATING FOR MY CHILD?

As soon as parents have a concern about the child's development, then it is time for the parents to begin advocating. Initially this may mean that the parents take time to speak with the teacher or the pediatrician about concerns for the child's development. It can also mean seeking a referral to get a child evaluated. Some doctors or teachers may not have the same concerns as the parents, but it is important for all parents to remember that they are the experts about the child. If the parents have a sincere concern, then it is important to get others to listen and take those concerns seriously. In order for advocate parents to learn to be question askers, they must think back to their own elementary school English classes and about how to create questions. The parents need to have lists of questions that include who, what, when, where, how, and why in order to learn about every aspect of a child's education.

- Who will be providing services to my child?
- When will my child receive support services?
- Where will my child receive therapy?
- What does the team want my child to learn during therapy?
- How will the therapist assess if my child is learning new skills from therapy?
- How can I assist the therapist and the teacher to help my child meet his goals?

The parent is also responsible for being an advocate for the child on the Admissions and Release Committee (ARC) or on the IEP team. It is the family members' job to share the family's top priorities with the rest of the committee. If it is important to the family that the entire family goes out to eat dinner together at restaurants frequently, then the committee may need to set a goal for a child to be able to feed herself independently. If it is very important to the family to attend weekly activities such as a church group or a supper club, then the IFSP team may focus on decreasing separation anxiety so the child can stay in the church childcare or with a babysitter. The family must advocate for goals that will help the child during daily life.

## DO I NEED TO LEARN ABOUT CERTAIN LAWS?

It is very important for any family that has a child with a developmental delay to learn about the national and state laws that ensure the child has rights and receives services. The most important law for parents to learn is the Individuals with Disabilities Education Act (IDEA) and the revisions made in 2004 that updated that title to the Individuals with Disabilities Education Improvement Act. These laws require every child to be given the right, by the state, to a free and appropriate education. These acts have also given parents and guardians the right to be involved in the planning of the child's educational goals. The family should be just as involved in the child's education team as any of the specialists.

When a child does not qualify for an IEP, but he or she still has a disability, delay, or a medical condition, then that child may qualify for services under the Rehabilitation Act of 1973 under section 504. This is another important law with which families should become comfortable. In order to qualify for a 504 Plan, the child must have a physical or mental impairment that significantly limits at least one major life activity. The key to advocating for a child using these laws is to study and understand the vocabulary. For a 504 Plan, the parent must understand what a "major life activity" is in order to make sure the child receives support services.

## WHAT ARE ADVOCACY STRATEGIES THAT FAMILIES NEED TO USE?

1. Establish relationships with teachers, therapists, and anyone who works with the child. Parents need to smile and greet the teachers any time they see them at school or in the community. It is important to establish a connection in some way. Instead of being just another parent at an ARC meeting, make yourself known for something. Be the parent who constantly says thank you to the staff or who brings brownies to the teachers' lounge. Parents should try to find something that they have in common with the therapists so they can have a personal conversation about books they have both read or trips they enjoy taking. The key for the family is to make the teachers and therapists comfortable around the family and speak with the parents over little concerns, as well as annual meetings. The teachers are more likely to tell parents upcoming changes and recommendations in a casual setting and explain those impacts if they already have an established relationship.

2. Spend time learning parent and child rights. Each child with a developmental delay or disability has rights under the IDEA education act and under the Americans with Disabilities Act. Very few parents realize that if the public school system cannot provide the type of education that the child needs, then the school system will be responsible for the cost of placing a child in the most appropriate educational placement. There are little parts of

these laws that provide children with a wide variety of opportunities, but to ensure that children receive every benefit, the parents must become experts on the law.

3. Don't be afraid to ask "why" questions during meetings. If the IEP team is creating a plan, the parents need to ask why questions as the specialists determine resources and objectives. If the school determines that the child can receive speech, then a parent advocate needs to push and ask why her child is only receiving thirty minutes of speech per week instead of an hour. If the team decides that the child should be pulled out of the classroom for occupational therapy, then the parent advocate needs to ask why the therapy can't occur in the natural classroom setting. When the IEP team says, "This is the way we have always done it," the parent advocate needs to ask why it can't be done a different way. The advocate must push the rest of the team to problem solve.

4. Keep your title as the expert. No one knows a child better than the parents. Many different experts sit down at a table during an IEP or IFSP meeting. The list typically includes experts on education, experts on special education, experts on child development, experts on medicine, experts on therapy, and experts on evaluation. The parents must remember that they are the experts on the child, and no one else at the table has that title. If the parent advocates are the experts about the child, they cannot give that power to the other team members. The team is there to support the family. The team shares expert information from their field, and then the family members can select the strategies that will help the child the most. It is important for all parent advocates to work cooperatively with the team, but it is essential for the parent to establish the title of the child expert.

5. Be prepared to get a second opinion. The school system teachers and therapists are licensed and certified in their fields, but that does not mean they always provide the best services. School therapists may be overworked by a large caseload and not be able to give the individual attention to each child that he or she needs. A child may not be accustomed to the teaching philosophy of a new teacher, so there could be some friction. If something is not working for the child, the parent advocate should always be will-

ing to get a second opinion. That may mean the parent gets the child an independent evaluation from a certified specialist outside the school system, or the parent may just reach out to an administrator or another member of the therapy team to see if small changes can be made in the classroom setting. The parents must always try to find what is best for their child, even if it isn't the first recommendation.

6. Don't worry about what others think. When families are new to early intervention and special education, they often don't want to make waves. They may occasionally look away when their children receive poor services because they don't want to be seen as a difficult parent. If parents must make a decision between keeping others happy and getting their child the best possible education, the parents should always decide in favor of the child. A good relationship with the teachers and the school is an asset, but if the school is not meeting the requirements established in the IEP, then it is time to voice a concern. Ultimately, the parent that speaks up is the parent who will get the school's attention.

7. Don't be afraid to ask for accommodations. Of course, there are some accommodations that the school or the therapy office does not have the financial resources to make; however, the parent will never know without asking. If no one makes the request, then additional services may never be offered. Ask for one-on-one time with an assistant in the classroom if the child has a significant disability. The worst thing that can happen is the IEP team denies the request. Ask for the child to have more time with the speech therapist if that is the predominant developmental concern. Ask for the child to be placed in a smaller classroom if the child needs more attention or struggles with overstimulation. Ask for a scribe if an elementary school child still has difficulty writing. Parents need to look at the child's developmental needs and consider what would benefit the child the most in a classroom or therapy setting. The worst thing that can happen is that the parent is told no.

8. Take advantage of community. Families of children with developmental delays must attend doctors' appointments, therapy sessions, and meetings to discuss child progress. It can be a huge asset for a parent to have a friend or family member go to the

doctor's office and simply be a calming presence. An ARC meeting can be intimidating for many parents, but it is important for the family to remember that they do not have to attend the meeting alone. The family can bring an advocate to the meeting to help them request services or to help explain the child's needs. When a family sits across the table from a team of specialists, it is easy to feel outnumbered. Another person who is there simply to support the family can allow the family the confidence they need to have challenging conversations.

## WHAT DOES THE WORLD NEED TO KNOW ABOUT MY CHILD?

The parent advocate actually has a specific assignment. The job of the advocate is to determine what the world needs to know about the child. When a child is diagnosed with a developmental delay, then the school or the therapist knows the child by that delay and the treatment plan that the child needs. The job of the parent advocate is to make sure the teachers and specialists learn about the whole child. What makes the child unique? What are the child's strengths? What motivates the child? What victories has the child already experienced?

The parent advocate also needs to establish long-term goals for the child and the family. This means that the parents really need to look toward the future and envision what the child is capable of doing. What type of independence will the child have in the future? Does the family want the child to pursue further education, hold a job, give back to the community, or even get married? Once the family can envision long-term goals for the child, then it is essential to communicate those goals again and again to the IEP team, the teachers, and the therapists.

If the parent wants the child to have an independent lifestyle when he or she leaves the public school system, then what types of goals does the child need to work toward? If the family wants the child to have the option to pursue further education after high school, then what type of goals need to be set in kindergarten and elementary school so the child will be successful in the future?

## SPEAKING UP WITHOUT TURNING PEOPLE OFF

Parent advocacy requires the family members to speak their minds and fight for the rights of their children. At the same time, it is important to continue positive working relationships whenever possible. One of the keys to keeping successful working relationships with teachers, therapists, and pediatricians is to listen sincerely to each expert's opinion.

Just as the family members have a desire to be heard, the professionals that work with the children are often working hard to serve each child in the best way possible. They have a passion for what they do, and they want their opinions to be considered respectfully. At the same time, the family is the guardian of the child, so they have a right to disagree with the recommendations of the teachers and specialists.

When seven or eight people sit down at a meeting to make decisions for a child, it is obvious that there may be differences in opinion. Despite those differences, the team can continue to work together successfully if everyone makes an effort to listen to each person's input and observations.

It is also important for family members to remember that there is a difference in being assertive and being hostile. Once a team member begins yelling or making accusations, it is very hard to keep a successful working relationship. Parents need to remember to be persistent, but they need to place a high priority on having an open mind and valuing calm conversations.

## GOING FORWARD

The ultimate goals for all parents are to take care of their children and provide them with the best possible education. To provide any child with quality health care and a quality education is hard work, but when a child has a diagnosed developmental delay, it becomes much more challenging. Once a parent realizes that his or her child needs additional assistance, that should be the parent's call to action. Pursue an evaluation and early intervention as soon as possible. If the professionals assisting the child don't understand the extent of the problems, then the parent needs to keep explaining the story until they do understand. Each parent needs to do research on the child's delay and on special education laws. Families need to prepare to work hard in therapy and fight hard against the health insurance companies. The early intervention process can be overwhelming, but at the end of the day, all of the hard work will help the child. That is what makes it worthwhile!

# ABOUT THE AUTHOR

**Sarah Taylor Vanover** has been working in the field of early childhood for more than nineteen years. She first began as an assistant teacher in an infant room, and since then she has served as a lead teacher, a program administrator, a trainer, and a classroom teaching coach. Vanover has also had the opportunity to work at the state level to assist with policy development and supervise early childhood trainers throughout the Commonwealth of Kentucky. She is currently the director of a Bright Horizons childcare program in Georgetown, Kentucky.

Vanover completed her doctoral research on what families look for when selecting childcare for their children. She is an active trainer in Kentucky and surrounding states, and she frequently speaks at conferences on topics such as quality childcare indicators, language development in the early childhood classroom, and the importance of quality infant and toddler care in early childhood education. For the past several years, Vanover has focused her work and research on assessing quality early childhood programs for health and safety requirements and school readiness skills.

Vanover lives in Lexington, Kentucky, with her husband, Rob, and their two sons, Jack and James.